INTRODUCING
ISSUES WITH
OPPOSING
VIEWPOINTS®

Welfare

Cynthia A. Bily, *Book Editor*

GREENHAVEN PRESS
A part of Gale, Cengage Learning

GALE
CENGAGE Learning™

Detroit • New York • San Francisco • New Haven, Conn • Waterville, Maine • London

Christine Nasso, *Publisher*
Elizabeth Des Chenes, *Managing Editor*

© 2009 Greenhaven Press, a part of Gale, Cengage Learning

For more information, contact:
Greenhaven Press
27500 Drake Rd.
Farmington Hills, MI 48331-3535
Or you can visit our Internet site at gale.cengage.com

For product information and technology assistance, contact us at

Gale Customer Support, 1-800-877-4253
For permission to use material from this text or product, submit all requests online at
www.cengage.com/permissions

Further permissions questions can be emailed to permissionrequest@cengage.com

Articles in Greenhaven Press anthologies are often edited for length to meet page requirements. In addition, original titles of these works are changed to clearly present the main thesis and to explicitly indicate the author's opinion. Every effort is made to ensure that Greenhaven Press accurately reflects the original intent of the authors. Every effort has been made to trace the owners of copyrighted material.

Cover image © Brooks Kraft/Sygma/Corbis

LIBRARY OF CONGRESS CATALOGING-IN-PUBLICATION DATA

Welfare / Cynthia A. Bily, editor.
    p. cm. -- (Introducing issues with opposing viewpoints)
  Includes bibliographical references and index.
  ISBN 978-0-7377-4485-9 (hardcover)
 1. Public welfare--United States--Juvenile literature. I. Bily, Cynthia A.
  HV95.W45 2009
  362.5'568--dc22

                                                                    2009012038

Printed in the United States of America
1 2 3 4 5 6 7 13 12 11 10 09

Contents

Foreword

Indulging in a wide spectrum of ideas, beliefs, and perspectives is a critical cornerstone of democracy. After all, it is often debates over differences of opinion, such as whether to legalize abortion, how to treat prisoners, or when to enact the death penalty, that shape our society and drive it forward. Such diversity of thought is frequently regarded as the hallmark of a healthy and civilized culture. As the Reverend Clifford Schutjer of the First Congregational Church in Mansfield, Ohio, declared in a 2001 sermon, "Surrounding oneself with only like-minded people, restricting what we listen to or read only to what we find agreeable is irresponsible. Refusing to entertain doubts once we make up our minds is a subtle but deadly form of arrogance." With this advice in mind, Introducing Issues with Opposing Viewpoints books aim to open readers' minds to the critically divergent views that comprise our world's most important debates.

Introducing Issues with Opposing Viewpoints simplifies for students the enormous and often overwhelming mass of material now available via print and electronic media. Collected in every volume is an array of opinions that captures the essence of a particular controversy or topic. Introducing Issues with Opposing Viewpoints books embody the spirit of nineteenth-century journalist Charles A. Dana's axiom: "Fight for your opinions, but do not believe that they contain the whole truth, or the only truth." Absorbing such contrasting opinions teaches students to analyze the strength of an argument and compare it to its opposition. From this process readers can inform and strengthen their own opinions, or be exposed to new information that will change their minds. Introducing Issues with Opposing Viewpoints is a mosaic of different voices. The authors are statesmen, pundits, academics, journalists, corporations, and ordinary people who have felt compelled to share their experiences and ideas in a public forum. Their words have been collected from newspapers, journals, books, speeches, interviews, and the Internet, the fastest growing body of opinionated material in the world.

Introducing Issues with Opposing Viewpoints shares many of the well-known features of its critically acclaimed parent series, Opposing Viewpoints. The articles are presented in a pro/con format, allowing readers to absorb divergent perspectives side by side. Active reading questions preface each viewpoint, requiring the student to approach the material thoughtfully and carefully. Useful charts, graphs, and cartoons supplement each article. A thorough introduction provides readers with crucial background on an issue. An annotated bibliography points the reader toward articles, books, and Web sites that contain additional information on the topic. An appendix of organizations to contact contains a wide variety of charities, nonprofit organizations, political groups, and private enterprises that each hold a position on the issue at hand. Finally, a comprehensive index allows readers to locate content quickly and efficiently.

Introducing Issues with Opposing Viewpoints is also significantly different from Opposing Viewpoints. As the series title implies, its presentation will help introduce students to the concept of opposing viewpoints and learn to use this material to aid in critical writing and debate. The series' four-color, accessible format makes the books attractive and inviting to readers of all levels. In addition, each viewpoint has been carefully edited to maximize a reader's understanding of the content. Short but thorough viewpoints capture the essence of an argument. A substantial, thought-provoking essay question placed at the end of each viewpoint asks the student to further investigate the issues raised in the viewpoint, compare and contrast two authors' arguments, or consider how one might go about forming an opinion on the topic at hand. Each viewpoint contains sidebars that include at-a-glance information and handy statistics. A Facts About section located in the back of the book further supplies students with relevant facts and figures.

Following in the tradition of the Opposing Viewpoints series, Greenhaven Press continues to provide readers with invaluable exposure to the controversial issues that shape our world. As John Stuart Mill once wrote: "The only way in which a human being can make some approach to knowing the whole of a subject is by hearing what can be said about it by persons of every variety of opinion and studying all modes in which it can be looked at by every character of mind. No wise man ever acquired his wisdom in any mode but this." It is to this principle that Introducing Issues with Opposing Viewpoints books are dedicated.

Introduction

"Our food banks are calling us every day, telling us that demand for emergency food is higher than it has ever been in our history. They are serving a significant number of new clients—people who were once their donors, middle class workers who can no longer make ends meet."

—Vicki Escarra, president and chief executive officer of Feeding America

In mid-November 2008, the U.S. Department of Agriculture (USDA) announced statistics that confirmed what many people already suspected: Americans in record numbers were going hungry. In 2007 the department declared that nearly one in eight Americans—more than 36 million adults and children—had struggled to obtain enough food to lead active, healthy lives, and almost 12 million had actually gone hungry during the year. This included 691,000 children who went hungry in 2007—the largest figure in a decade. In the government's official terminology, these people were classified as having "very low food security."

As troubling as these figures were, experts warned that due to the economic crisis spreading across the globe during the second half of 2008, the number of Americans living in poverty could only increase. "There's every reason to think the increases in the number of hungry people will be very, very large," said James Weill, president of the Food Research and Action Center, "based on the increased demand we're seeing this year at food stamp agencies, emergency kitchens, Women, Infants and Children clinics, really across the entire social service support structure." In fact, in December 2008 the USDA released a report saying that because of rising unemployment and increases in the price of food, 30 million Americans had received food stamps the month before—the largest number since the program began.

Many observed that the United States had not seen so many people in financial trouble since the Great Depression, when the programs that are commonly called "welfare" were created. Until that time, there was no organized effort by the federal government to help the poor. There were state-sponsored projects in some states, and churches and civic groups and neighbors offered support, and people worked hard—when work was available—to feed their families, but it became clear that only a national program could reach everyone, wherever they lived, whatever their faith, whatever their need. President Franklin Delano Roosevelt created the social welfare programs that he called the New Deal between 1933 and 1936, saying, "The test of our progress is not whether we add more to the abundance of those who have much. It is whether we provide enough for those who have little."

"Welfare" in the twenty-first century generally refers to any of six programs funded by the federal and state governments: Temporary Assistance for Needy Families (TANF), which provides up to five years of financial support to working adults; the Supplemental Nutrition Assistance Program, more commonly known as "food stamps"; the Housing Choice Voucher Program, known as "Section 8," which helps families pay rent; Medicaid, which funds medical care; Supplemental Security Income, which provides cash assistance to people who are elderly, blind, or disabled; and unemployment insurance, which gives cash assistance to people who lose their jobs. New economic realities and new understandings of how to help have led Congress to adjust and revamp the programs several times, most notably in the 1960s, when food stamps and Medicaid were created, and the 1990s, when "welfare reform" introduced new regulations intended to make welfare recipients more responsible for helping themselves.

Not everyone believes that welfare is a good idea. Many have argued that people who receive welfare come to depend on these programs and forget how to take care of themselves. Columnist Joel Hilliker calls this dependency "poisonous," arguing that the effects of welfare "can include decreased sense of individual responsibility, degraded work ethic, the fragmentation of families, and a sense of entitlement that engenders selfishness, thanklessness and unhappiness." Robert Rector, who has long argued for reductions in welfare programs, believes that many people who receive aid do not need it. "Most poor children today," he comments, "are, in fact, supernourished and grow up to be, on average, one inch taller and 10 pounds heavier than the GIs [soldiers] who stormed the beaches of Normandy in World War II." But others, including Barack Obama, who was elected in 2008, replacing George W. Bush as president of the United States, see it differently. During his campaign, Obama pledged to eliminate child hunger in the United States by 2015, and declared that accomplishing this goal would require a commitment from the federal government. "Improving and expanding federal food assistance and nutrition programs," he said, "will . . . be a key component of ending hunger in the United States."

Although the programs have changed since the New Deal, what has not changed is the controversy over how best to help people who are struggling. Economists disagree about the most efficient ways to spend government dollars, religious groups and other private organizations disagree about whether they should take on more or less of the responsibility of helping their neighbors, taxpayers disagree about how much of the burden they should shoulder, and welfare recipients and their advocates disagree about whether the programs help or hurt low-income people. As people of good will work to determine the best role for government in helping poor citizens, they must struggle with three important questions: Does Welfare Serve Needy Groups Fairly? Has Welfare Reform Been Successful? Are There Good Alternatives to Welfare? The authors of the following viewpoints present a range of answers to these questions.

Chapter 1

Does Welfare Serve Needy Groups Fairly?

A low-income family in Texas lives in squalid conditions and must cope with minimal indoor plumbing.

Welfare Rules Make Life Harder for Single Mothers

"The number of single mothers who are unemployed and who receive no welfare assistance has doubled."

Allison Stevens

In the following viewpoint Allison Stevens argues that welfare reform, which was intended to help people get jobs and support themselves, has actually made it more difficult for many women to provide for their families. She contends that the new laws have been particularly hard on women. Even though many single mothers have found jobs under welfare reform, she concludes, most of these jobs do not pay enough to lift them out of poverty. Stevens is Washington bureau chief for the nonprofit independent news service Women's eNews, where this viewpoint originally appeared.

AS YOU READ, CONSIDER THE FOLLOWING QUESTIONS:

1. Why did voters in Wisconsin decide to make their assistance programs less generous in the 1980s, according to the viewpoint?
2. Which three groups of women have the highest poverty rates, as reported in the viewpoint?
3. Why, according to the author, are economic downturns harder on women than on men?

In 2001, Lisa Craig snuck out of her home in Chicago and boarded a bus for Milwaukee with her three children, leaving behind an abusive husband, a stable job and most of her possessions.

The elimination in 1996 of federal welfare entitlements had its roots here in Wisconsin, where voters in the 1980s were angered over perceptions that poor Chicago "welfare queens" were heading north to take advantage of more generous programs. But Craig headed north because she had family there to help her.

After a short stay with her sister, Craig took her children—aged 1 to 8—to a homeless shelter. In order to receive a monthly welfare payment of about $600, she entered a three-month training program with the hope of landing a job at the end of it.

But the training didn't pay off. She didn't find full-time employment until 2006, when she was hired as a retail clerk at Goodwill, which paid enough to cover her $600 rent but not much else. The job lasted only until November [2007] and she has been looking for another since.

Over the years, Craig has made ends meet with the help of Wisconsin Works, or W2, the state's overhauled welfare system. But she is "disenchanted" with the program because it has not lived up to its promise

Clay Bennett, *The Christian Science Monitor.*

of helping her obtain long-term employment. "They need to come up with something else," she said in an interview.

Craig is caught in the public policy experiments that began in Milwaukee in 1987 when Gov. Tommy Thompson tied welfare payments to behavior, including requiring recipients to engage in work-related activities, not need. Thompson stiffened the requirements in 1994. The country took notice as Wisconsin welfare rolls plummeted.

In 1996, President Bill Clinton teamed up with a Republican Congress to enact the Personal Responsibility and Work Opportunity Reconciliation Act, a welfare overhaul reflecting much of the new policies in Wisconsin. The law was reauthorized in 2006.

Advocates working on behalf of single mothers say the law, which ended government's obligation to provide minimum support to impoverished single heads of households, has exacerbated poverty.

"It definitely has played a role in the demise of the city," said Sangita Nayak, an organizer with 9 to 5 National Association of Working Women, an advocacy group based here.

> **FAST FACT**
>
> Of the low-income parents with no employment during 2006, 42 percent reported that they were not working because they were taking care of their families, according to the National Center for Children in Poverty.

U.S. Women and Poverty

In 2006, 12 percent of Wisconsin women lived in poverty, compared to 9.7 percent of men, according to census data.

Advocates see some rays of hope that life will improve for the city's poor. In April [2008], voters elected the only woman to the 15-member city council; in May, a philanthropist gave $50 million to boost low-income neighborhoods; and in June, the state opened a new department to improve the life of children and families.

But without the welfare benefits, poor women are giving up on government to help them survive, said Joyce Mallory, a former program director at the Wisconsin Council on Children and Families in Madison. "A lot of people just stop trying," she said. "They just figure, 'Hey, I'll try to get by. I'll do whatever I have to do.'"

Single Mothers: Work and Welfare, 1996–2005

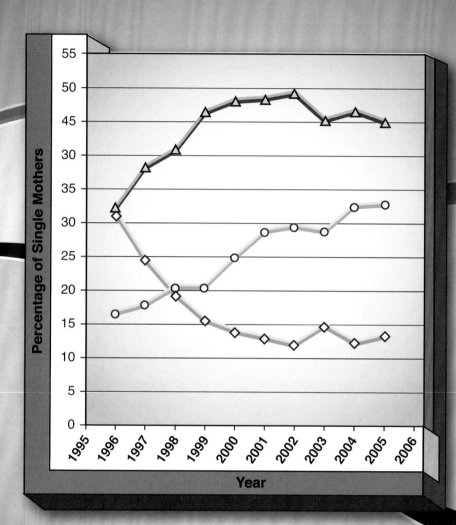

Note: Percentage of single mothers who worked *and* received cash benefits over the year dropped from 20.3 percent in 1996 to 8.9 percent in 2005.

Some 15 million U.S. women live in poverty, according to 2006 Census data collated by the Washington-based National Women's Law Center. Poverty rates are especially high among women of color, older women and single mothers. Black and Hispanic women are about twice as likely to be poor than white women. Roughly 1 in 5 elderly women are poor, as are 1 in 3 single mothers.

For many, poverty has worsened in recent years due to the shrinking economy, higher unemployment rates and the rising cost of fuel and food.

That is especially true in Milwaukee, now the seventh poorest city in the nation. Here, temporary homeless shelters have become permanent, food pantries are pleading for donations to meet demand and public schools now serve universal free breakfasts, Mallory said.

Like many other cities in the Rust Belt—the swath of industrial states that stretch from the Northeast through the Midwest—Milwaukee has seen a steady loss of jobs, many in the decent-paying manufacturing sector.

Economic Downturns Hit Women Hardest

Economic downturns hit women the hardest because they earn less than men; are more likely to work part-time; are less likely to be eligible for unemployment insurance; are less likely to have health insurance; and are more likely to leave their jobs because of caregiving responsibilities, domestic violence, or harassment or stalking.

Since the welfare overhaul, the number of recipients plunged as many found stable employment. At the same time, the number of single mothers who are unemployed and who receive no welfare assistance has doubled, from 16 percent in 1996 to nearly 33 percent in 2005, or 1 in 3 single parents.

Wisconsin's welfare provides unemployed single heads of households with children payments of up to $673 a month and the parent must participate in at least 40 hours of assigned work, work-related activities or training programs a week. That averages to about $4.20 an hour, considerably below the current minimum wage . . . which is set to increase to $7.25 per hour [in] July [2009].

Parents can apply for county-based programs to help them pay for child care, medical treatment and food. Some parents can work part-time for pro-rated benefits.

INNER CITY EMPLOYMENT OFFICE 420173

Women are harder hit than men by economic downturns because they may earn less than men and are often ineligible for unemployment insurance.

Proponents say the effort to move people from welfare to work has been a tremendous success, helping parents—especially single mothers—find stable jobs to support their families. The welfare overhaul, they say, has also helped women collect child support.

"A Signal Achievement"

"Welfare reform stands as a signal achievement, in my judgment, in social reform policy," Secretary of Health and Human Services

Michael Leavitt said in a 2006 speech marking the law's 10th anniversary. "The act brought significant improvements in the lives of many Americans by helping them break the cycle of dependency and encouraging them to pursue self-sufficiency."

He pointed to a 57 percent decline in the national welfare caseload between 1996 and 2006.

Nowhere has that been more evident than in Wisconsin, where welfare participation has dropped from 90,000 in 1996 to 6,400 today, said Reggie Bicha, head of the state's Department of Children and Family Services. In 2007, over 5,000 participants found work, with an average hourly wage of $8.54.

But critics say the numbers don't tell the whole story.

More single mothers are employed now than were in the 1990s, according to Liz Schott, a welfare expert at the Washington-based Center on Budget and Policy Priorities.

But recent declines suggest a healthy economy—rather than changes to welfare—helps people transition to work, she said. And many of those now working are still poor because they do not earn enough to afford child care, transportation and other work expenses, she added.

Moreover, the government did not implement a mechanism to track those who left the system. Countless others are now homeless and living in extreme poverty, she added.

"This is going to catch up with us," Schott said. "We no longer have the very, very, very weak safety net that we used to have for poor families with children."

EVALUATING THE AUTHOR'S ARGUMENTS:

Unlike the author of the following viewpoint, Allison Stevens begins her argument with the story of an individual woman, Lisa Craig, who has tried unsuccessfully to support her children. Why do you think the author decided to begin her piece this way? How does reading Craig's story first affect the way you respond to the factual information later in the viewpoint?

Welfare Reform Has Helped Single Mothers

Kay S. Hymowitz

"The percentage of employed single mothers rose, in the years following reform."

In the following viewpoint Kay S. Hymowitz recalls what she considers misplaced fears about welfare reform, and contends that the reforms have, in fact, succeeded. Not only have women and children left the welfare rolls, she contends, but they have improved their economic status. Most women who have gotten off welfare, she concludes, have found jobs or other means of support. Hymowitz is the William E. Simon fellow at the Manhattan Institute and a contributing editor to the urban-policy magazine *City Journal*, where this viewpoint first appeared. She writes extensively on education and childhood in America.

AS YOU READ, CONSIDER THE FOLLOWING QUESTIONS:

1. When was the bill for welfare reform passed, as reported in the viewpoint?
2. As reported in the viewpoint, what was the name of the program that Temporary Assistance for Needy Families (TANF) replaced?
3. What percentage of working single mothers were earning minimum wage or less four years after they left welfare, according to research done by June O'Neill and Anne Hill?

Welfare reform celebrates its tenth anniversary this year [2006], and celebrates seems the right word. As most readers know, Temporary Assistance for Needy Families (TANF) ended the much-despised Depression-era federal entitlement to cash benefits for needy single mothers, replacing it with short-term, work-oriented programs designed and run by individual states. Its success has surprised just about everyone, supporters and naysayers alike.

So it seems a good time to remember the drama—make that melodrama—that the bill unleashed in 1996. Cries from Democrats of "anti-family," "anti-child," "mean-spirited," echoed through the Capitol, as did warnings of impending Third World–style poverty: "children begging for money, children begging for food, eight- and nine-year-old prostitutes," as New Jersey senator Frank Lautenberg put it. . . .

The Opposition's Mistaken Expectations

Before examining *why* so many people were wrong, let's look at exactly *how* they were wrong—an easy task, given the Everest of data on welfare reform's aftermath. TANF did not include a federal jobs program for the poor—though many wanted it to—but it has ended up being a WPA [Works Progress Administration—a 1930s federal jobs program] for social scientists, who have been busily crunching just about every number that happened to wander anywhere near a welfare recipient for the past ten years.

The most striking outcome has been the staggering decline in the welfare rolls, so large it has left even reform enthusiasts agog. At their peak in 1994—the rolls began to shrink before 1996, because many states had already instituted experimental reform programs—there were 5.1 million families on Aid to Families with Dependent Children, the old program. Almost immediately, the numbers went into freefall, and by 2004 they were down by 60 percent, to fewer than 2 million. . . .

Caseload declines are all well and good, but what caused opponents—and many proponents as well—to lose sleep was what would happen to women and their children once they left the dole. There were four chief concerns: First, would welfare leavers find jobs? Second, would they sink even deeper into poverty? Third, would their children be harmed? And fourth, would the states take advantage

In 1996 President Clinton signed into law the Temporary Assistance for Needy Families (TANF) Act designed to get people off welfare and into the workforce.

of the wide flexibility the bill gave them on implementation to join what many anticipated would be a "race to the bottom"?

Single Mothers Find Work

So let's consider concern number one: Did women who left the rolls actually go to work? The answer is: more than almost anyone had predicted. According to one Urban Institute study, 63 percent of leavers were working in the peak year of 1999. True, some studies showed numbers only in the high fifties, but even these findings were much better than expected.

Nevertheless, a lot of skeptics still weren't biting. It was the luck of a boom economy, they said; just wait until the job market sours. Well, the recession came in 2001, and though it was no picnic, it was—once again—nothing like what had been feared. As of 2002, 57 percent of leavers continued to punch a time clock. That, the critics warned, was only because the first recipients to leave welfare were likely to be the most competent. Just wait until we're dealing with the most dysfunctional, those who have the most "barriers to employment"—from limited education or work experience to English-language deficiency or mental disability.

But even there the news was encouraging. The Urban Institute kept a close eye on the caseload composition in welfare reform's early years and found that the proportion of highly disadvantaged women was no greater in 1999 than in 1997. A 2003 study by June O'Neill and Anne Hill found a large increase in the employment of some of these women: for example, in 1992 only 31 percent of young single mothers who were high school dropouts were employed; by 2000, 50 percent had jobs. And none of this takes into account the women who under the previous regime might have gone on welfare but, after TANF, with its time limits and hassles, never did. The percentage of employed single mothers rose, in the years following reform, from 45 percent in 1990 to 62 percent in 2005—nearing the employment rate of their married counterparts.

More Money than Before

What about concern number two—that welfare mothers would sink deeper into poverty? Shortly before TANF passed, the Urban Institute released a report, solicited by a wavering [President Bill] Clinton administration, warning that welfare reform could impoverish an additional 2 million people. Reform Jeremiahs waved the

FAST FACT

The U.S. Census Bureau reports that the poverty rate for single mothers fell from 42 to 36 percent, a 14.3 percent decline, between 1996 and 2004.

report around as scientific proof of their worst fears. Even if some welfare mothers did find jobs, they argued, they would merely be stocking shelves at Duane Reade [pharmacy] or making hotel beds, the proverbial "dead-end jobs" that would leave them worse off than on the dole.

Though a lot of women did take low-paying service jobs, the unreformed got this one wrong, too. For one thing, they failed to consider the Earned Income Tax Credit, whose expansion in 1993 meant a 40 percent boost in annual earnings for a minimum-wage worker with two kids. Most leavers, though, were doing better than minimum

Employment Rates of Married and Never-Married Mothers

Percentage

80
70
60
50
40
30

Married

Never married

1978 1980   1990   2000 2005

Year

Taken from: Gary Burtless (Brookings Institution) / U.S. Bureau of Labor Statistics.
www.city-journal.org/assets/images/16_2_02.jpg.

wage. In 2002, the same Urban Institute that had predicted TANF disaster found that the median hourly wage for working former recipients was around $8 an hour. Moreover, O'Neill and Hill discovered that, just as with most other people, the longer recipients were in the job market, the more they earned; four years off welfare, only 4 percent of working single mothers—and only 8 percent of high school dropouts who were single mothers—were earning minimum wage or less.

As a result, most welfare leavers had more money than when they were on welfare. The poverty rate for single women with children fell from 42 percent in 1996 to 34 percent in 2002; before 1996, it had never in recorded history been below 40 percent. This was the first boom ever where poverty declined faster for that group than for married-couple families. Nor did leavers disdain their "dead-end jobs." Studies consistently found that ex-recipients who went on to become waitresses, grill cooks, and security guards took pride in being salarywomen.

Still, it's fair to say that while post-reform America did not look like Calcutta [destitute city in India], it was no low-wage worker's paradise, either, especially as the economy weakened in late 2001. Ex-welfare mothers were still poorer than single mothers overall. Some who worked had less income than on welfare. Many were not working full-time, and an estimated 40 percent of those who left the welfare rolls returned later on. In 1999, close to 10 percent of leavers were "disconnected"—neither working nor on welfare nor supported by a working spouse. By the recession year of 2002, that number had risen to almost 14 percent. From the beginning, studies from the Children's Defense Fund and the Center for Budget and Policy Priorities warned of an increase in the number of families in deep poverty, and a steady stream of rumors claimed that soup kitchens and homeless shelters had crowds of ex-recipients clamoring at their doors.

But at least some of these warnings turned out to have been yet more crying wolf. Those who returned to the dole tended soon to find other means of support, getting a new job, signing up for disability or unemployment insurance, or turning to employed partners.

EVALUATING THE AUTHOR'S ARGUMENTS:

The author of the viewpoint you have just read refers several times to what she considers the mistakes of those who disagree with her. She mentions the "drama—make that melodrama" of her opponents' earlier warnings, she considers explaining their errors "an easy task," and she refers to opponents as "Jeremiahs," or constant doomsayers. How does this approach affect the way you read the viewpoint? Explain your answer.

Welfare Should Do a Better Job of Helping Immigrants

"The overhaul of welfare in 1996 ... imposed restrictions on certain legal noncitizens' access to government services."

Nancy K. Cauthen and Kinsey Alden Dinan

In the following viewpoint Nancy K. Cauthen and Kinsey Alden Dinan argue that the government should pay more attention to the well-being of the children of immigrant parents. Many of them, the authors contend, live with parents who work hard but are still poor, and who struggle to obtain welfare benefits. The authors conclude that it is in the nation's economic as well as moral interest to help children by supporting immigrant families. Both of the authors work with the National Center for Children in Poverty, Cauthen as a political and historical sociologist, and Dinan as a senior policy analyst.

AS YOU READ, CONSIDER THE FOLLOWING QUESTIONS:

1. What percentage of children in the United States live in immigrant families, according to the viewpoint?
2. What is the meaning of the term "mixed status," as explained in the viewpoint?
3. What are some of the reasons that even many legal immigrants do not participate in benefit programs, according to the viewpoint?

W e have heard from the president [George W. Bush] and the House of Representatives on immigration reform. Now, the Senate Judiciary Committee is debating the issue, with the full Senate expecting a bill by the end of [March 2006]. Despite the reality that more than 20 percent of this nation's children live in immigrant families, the debate has largely ignored these children. We need national leadership that understands and cares about the needs of immigrant workers and their families.

Immigrant children, and the much larger group of children born in the U.S. of immigrant parents, are at great risk for living in poverty, which compromises their health, safety and futures. Living on the edge even as their parents work extremely hard, these children are less likely than other children to receive help from government programs that protect low-wage workers and their families.

This is a paradox we cannot continue to ignore. Assisting the children of immigrants is central to promoting the economic security of America's families.

Immigration and the Working Poor

Until recently, our country's immigrant population had been concentrated in six states: California, Florida, Illinois, New Jersey, New York and Texas. However, the 19 states that saw their foreign-born population more than double between 1990 and 2000 did not include any of these six "traditional" immigration states. Altogether, children of immigrants comprise more than 26 percent of all low-income children in the United States.

Yet virtually all immigrant families are working families. According to a report by the National Center for Children in Poverty, 97 percent of children with foreign-born parents have a parent who works and 72 percent have a parent who works full-time, year round. Despite high rates of employment, many immigrant parents struggle to provide for their children.

> **FAST FACT**
>
> The National Center for Children in Poverty reports that 57 percent of children whose parents are immigrants are low-income, compared to 35 percent of children whose parents were born in the United States.

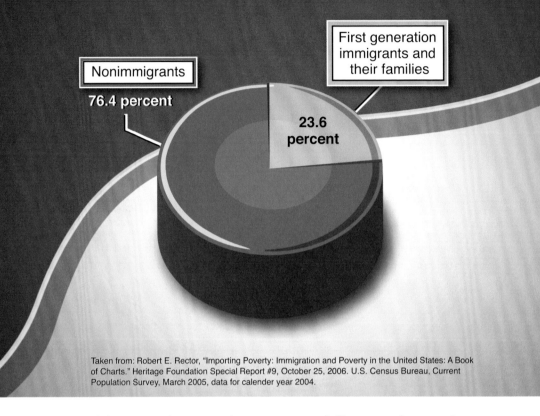

Taken from: Robert E. Rector, "Importing Poverty: Immigration and Poverty in the United States: A Book of Charts." Heritage Foundation Special Report #9, October 25, 2006. U.S. Census Bureau, Current Population Survey, March 2005, data for calender year 2004.

Addressing their needs means carefully considering the interplay of policies regarding immigration and the working poor. The bulk of immigrant families are considered "mixed status," with the majority of parents noncitizens while more than 70 percent of their children are full legal citizens. These same children are often held hostage by federal restrictions that limit their or family members' eligibility for important safety nets, such as food stamps and public health insurance.

Until about 10 years ago, most legal residents were eligible for public benefits just like American citizens. This changed with the overhaul of welfare in 1996, which imposed restrictions on certain legal noncitizens' access to government services designed to assist low-wage workers and their families. The upshot has been reduced benefit participation even among legal immigrants—citizens and residents alike—who remained eligible for assistance.

Protecting an Important Asset

Confusion over changed eligibility rules partly explains the drop, but fear of interacting with government officials is a big factor. Heightened penalties and stories of deportation in a more hostile climate post-9/11 [2001 terrorist attacks] have exacerbated immigrants' reluctance to seek assistance, compounding the impact of other cultural and linguistic barriers.

This country benefits immeasurably from the contributions of immigrants. We can and should do better.

According to the National Center for Children in Poverty, 97 percent of children born of immigrant parents have one parent who works, and 72 percent have a parent working full-time.

First, the federal government should eliminate eligibility restrictions based on citizenship status. These restrictions penalize hardworking families and jeopardize the futures of millions of children. Policymakers should increase the opportunities for undocumented immigrants to gain legal status and grant their children access to public health insurance and other benefits.

To meet immediate human needs, some states address the gap in supports by offering their own programs for legal noncitizens who are barred from federal benefits. State policies that promote family economic security more generally are also essential for assisting immigrant families.

In industrialized countries across Europe, governments are concerned that as their populations age, the ultimate resource—human capital—becomes scarce. But America has the promise of a still growing country of young people, and we need to recognize that they are our greatest potential asset. The vast majority of the children of immigrants will remain here for life. Opportunities for our future will depend on the opportunities we afford them.

EVALUATING THE AUTHORS' ARGUMENTS:

Both the viewpoint you have just read and the one you are about to read discuss how supporting immigrants affects native-born Americans and the nation as a whole. Cauthen and Dinan argue that protecting children—even those who are immigrants or whose parents are immigrants—is important to the economic future of the country. Schlafly argues that the cost of supporting immigrants is eroding the economic security of the country. How should citizens and government officials weigh these issues? How should a nation measure how many people it can afford to help?

Welfare Should Not Be Used to Support Immigrants

"Attempts to limit welfare eligibility for illegal aliens by provisions added to the 1996 welfare reform law . . . all failed."

Phyllis Schlafly

In the following viewpoint Phyllis Schlafly outlines the expenses associated with providing welfare and other support to immigrants in the United States. Immigrants today, she contends, are different from those who arrived in the early twentieth century because they are less likely to support themselves and more likely to receive government assistance. The high costs associated with supporting immigrants, she concludes, affect the well-being of everyone. Schlafly is a conservative political activist known primarily for opposing feminism. She is founder and president of the Eagle Forum, which supports American sovereignty and identity.

AS YOU READ, CONSIDER THE FOLLOWING QUESTIONS:

1. What is the meaning of the term "working poor," as explained in the viewpoint?
2. According to the viewpoint, what percentage of immigrants in the U.S. workforce did not have a high school education in 2005?
3. What has happened to emergency rooms in Los Angeles, as reported in the viewpoint?

Phyllis Schlafly, "A New Argument About Immigration," EagleForum.com, May 28, 2008. Reproduced by permission of the author.

Many arguments, pro and con, about how to deal with illegal aliens have been passionately debated over the past couple of years, but there are still other arguments that need public exposure. Mark Krikorian presents a new argument in his forthcoming book called *The New Case Against Immigration: Both Legal and Illegal.*

The pro-more-immigration crowd argues that today's immigrants are just like immigrants of a century ago: poor people looking for a better life who are expected to advance in our land of opportunity. Krikorian's new argument is that while today's immigrants may be like earlier ones, the America they come to is so very different that our previous experience with immigrants is practically irrelevant.

The essential difference between the two waves of immigrants was best summed up by the Nobel Prize–winning advocate of a free market, Milton Friedman. He said, "It's just obvious that you can't have free immigration and a welfare state."

The term "welfare state" does not just mean handouts to the non-working. Our welfare state encompasses dozens of social programs that provide benefits to the "working poor," *i.e.*, people working for wages low enough that they pay little or no income taxes.

Immigration Then and Now

Immigrants of the previous generation were expected to earn their own living, pay taxes like everybody else, learn our language, love America, and assimilate into our culture. Today's immigrants likewise come here for jobs not welfare.

During those prior major waves of immigration, the United States didn't have a welfare state. Native-born Americans survived the Great Depression of the 1930s without a welfare state.

The Social Security retirement system was established only in 1935. Most other agencies that redistribute cash and costly benefits from taxpayers to non-taxpayers started with [President] Lyndon Johnson's Great Society in the late 1960s.

Today's low-wage immigrants and lower-wage illegals can't earn what it costs to live in modern America, so they supplement with means-tested taxpayer benefits. And many immigrants don't learn our language or assimilate into American culture because of the multicultural diversity taught in our schools and encouraged in our society.

Immigrants of previous generations were expected to earn their own living, pay taxes, learn English, and assimilate into the American culture.

Today's immigrants fit the profile of the people who benefit from our welfare state: the working poor with large families. Krikorian sets forth some dismal figures.

About 30 percent of all immigrants in the U.S. workforce in 2005 lacked a high school education, which is four times the rate for native-born Americans. Among the largest group of working-age immigrants, the Mexicans, 62 percent have less than a high-school education, which means they work low-wage jobs.

Nearly half of immigrant households, 45 percent, are in or near poverty compared with 29 percent of native-headed households. Among Mexicans living in the United States, nearly two-thirds live in or near the government's definition of poverty.

Supporting Immigrants Is Costly

Costly social benefits provided to the working poor include Temporary Assistance [for] Needy Families (now called TANF, formerly AFDC [Aid for Families with Dependent Children]), food stamps, school lunches, Medicaid, WIC (nutrition for Women, Infants and Children), public housing, and Supplemental Security Income (SSI).

The Earned Income Tax Credit (EITC) is one of the most expensive parts of income redistribution. Twice as many immigrant households (30 percent) qualify for this cash handout as native-headed households (15 percent).

Health care is another huge cost. Nearly half of immigrants are either uninsured or on Medicaid, which is nearly double the rate for native-born families. Federal law requires hospitals to treat all comers to emergency rooms, even if uninsured and unable to pay.

Hospitals try to shift the costs onto their paying patients, and when the hospitals exhaust their ability to do this, they close their doors. In Los Angeles, 60 hospitals have closed their emergency rooms over the past decade, which imposes another kind of cost.

Immigration accounts for nearly all the growth in elementary and secondary school enrollment over the past generation. The children of immigrants now comprise 19 percent of the school-age population and 21 percent of the preschool population.

The Heritage Foundation estimated that in order to reduce government payments to the average low-skill household to a level equal to

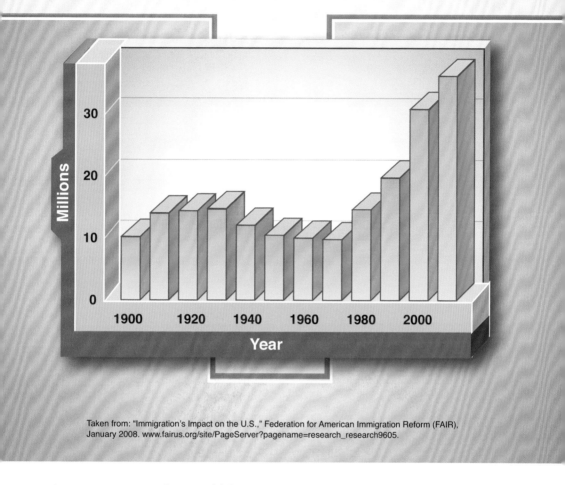

Taken from: "Immigration's Impact on the U.S.," Federation for American Immigration Reform (FAIR), January 2008. www.fairus.org/site/PageServer?pagename=research_research9605.

the taxes it pays, "it would be necessary to eliminate Social Security and Medicare, all means-tested welfare, and to cut expenditures on public education roughly in half." Obviously, that is not going to happen.

Attempts to limit welfare eligibility for illegal aliens by provisions added to the 1996 welfare reform law, SSI, food stamps, Medicaid and TANF all failed. Krikorian concludes that "Walling immigrants off from government benefits once we've let them in is a fantasy."

As Americans are pinched between falling real estate values and the inflation of necessities such as gasoline, they are entitled to know how their tax dollars are being spent. The big bite that social benefits to immigrants (one-third of whom are illegal) takes out of taxpayers' paychecks should be factored into any debate about immigration or amnesty policy.

EVALUATING THE AUTHOR'S ARGUMENTS:

In the viewpoint you have just read, Phyllis Schlafly makes several references to immigrants of the past. For example, she writes that "Immigrants of the previous generation were expected to earn their own living, pay taxes like everyone else, learn our language, love America, and assimilate." She does not state directly whether she believes immigrants today are like or unlike this description. Why not? How does her strategy of implying comparisons without stating them directly affect how you read the viewpoint?

Chapter 2

Has Welfare Reform Been Successful?

New Jersey governor Jon S. Corzine signs legislation to create the Department of Children and Family as part of welfare reform in 2006.

Welfare Reform Has Helped People Escape Poverty

"The overall poverty rate fell from 14.5 percent in 1994 to 11.3 percent in 2000."

Lawrence M. Mead

In the following viewpoint, which was originally presented as testimony before the U.S. Congress, Lawrence M. Mead contends that the most important reason many people live in poverty is that they do not have paying jobs. He argues that welfare reform, by requiring more people to work, has led to more people finding jobs and moving away from poverty without making their lives more difficult. As the government makes adjustments to its policies to further reduce poverty, he concludes, it should continue its successful work requirements. Mead is a professor of politics at New York University and specializes in welfare policy and reform.

AS YOU READ, CONSIDER THE FOLLOWING QUESTIONS:
1. What does the author mean by the phrase "help and hassle," as used in the viewpoint?
2. Which government program provides wage subsidies for low-wage workers, as reported in the viewpoint?
3. In the viewpoint, how does the author characterize the overall economic conditions of the 1990s?

Lawrence M. Mead, "Testimony," U.S. House Committee on Ways and Means, April 26, 2007. Reproduced by permission of the author.

I am a Professor of Politics at New York University and a longtime scholar of antipoverty policy and welfare reform. I've written several books on these subjects, including a study of welfare reform in Wisconsin. I appreciate this chance to testify on an important question: What should government do next to reduce poverty in America?

The main conclusions of my research might be summarized as follows:

- *Nonwork by parents is the main reason for poverty among the working-aged* and their children. Family breakup is also important but secondary.
- *Nonwork cannot generally be explained by barriers* to employment such as lack of jobs or child care. Barriers—particularly inferior education—have much more influence on the quality of jobs people get *if* they work.
- *Nonwork cannot be overcome by voluntary measures alone,* such as greater investments in child care, education, or training. These are of value mostly after nonworkers have entered jobs.

In 2002 President George W. Bush talks about his efforts to renew legislation for the welfare reform bill that increased work requirements for welfare recipients.

- *Rather, work levels can be raised by a combination of "help and hassle"*—new benefits coupled with requirements that poor adults work as a condition of aid.
- *Work enforcement is ultimately a political process* where stronger work expectations coupled with new benefits cause more poor adults to go to work without necessarily going on welfare at all.

The Success of Reform

In reforming welfare, government has largely followed this approach since enactment of the Family Support Act (FSA) in 1988, and especially since the enactment of the Personal Responsibility and Work Opportunity Reconciliation Act (PRWORA) in 1996. Under PRWORA, Temporary Assistance for Needy Families (TANF) replaced Aid to Families with Dependent Children (AFDC).

Tougher work requirements were combined with new spending on child and health care for families leaving welfare and on wage subsidies for low-paid workers (the Earned Income Tax Credit, or EITC).

These were the main effects:

- *A dramatic fall in dependency:* Since their height in 1994, the rolls in AFDC/TANF have plummeted by over 60 percent. Nor did dependency rebound during the recession of 2001–3.
- *A substantial rise in work levels among single mothers:* The share of AFDC cases meeting work participation norms rose from 22 percent in 1994 to 38 percent in 1999, before falling to 32 percent by 2004. Work among poor single mothers also rose: The share working at all rose from 44 percent in 1993 to 64 percent in 1999, before falling to 54 percent in 2005. For work full-time and year-round, the comparable figures were 9, 17, and 16 percent.
- *A substantial fall in poverty:* The overall poverty rate fell from 14.5 percent in 1994 to 11.3 percent in 2000, before rising to 12.6 percent in 2005. For children, the equivalent figures are 21.8, 16.2, and 17.6 percent.

• *An absence of hardship due to reform:* Welfare reform did not generally make life tougher for poor families, although . . . it did not solve all their problems. The noneconomic effects of reform on families and children were small and largely positive.

Most analysts think that the main forces behind these gains were (1) the new work tests in welfare, (2) expanded support benefits—especially EITC—and (3) the superb economic conditions of the 1990s. There is some debate about the relative importance of these factors, but everyone thinks that work requirements were essential to forcing change.

Government should follow the same general approach as it seeks to reduce poverty further. Neither "help" nor "hassle" will achieve much without the other. Government should not extend new benefits

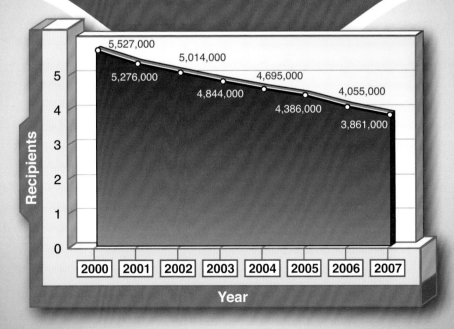

TANF Recipients Are Decreasing

Since the year 2000, the number of individuals receiving Temporary Assistance for Needy Families (TANF) benefits has steadily decreased.

Taken from: U.S. Department of Health and Human Services, 2000–2008. www.acf.hhs.gov/programs/ofa/data-reports/caseload/caseload_recent.html.

or opportunities to the employable poor without expecting work. Neither should it cut back spending, in an indirect attempt to force them to work. Rather, it should expect work directly while also providing the benefits people need to reorganize their lives around employment.

EVALUATING THE AUTHOR'S ARGUMENTS:

In the opening of the viewpoint you have just read, Lawrence M. Mead establishes his credentials as an expert on questions about poverty and welfare and explains that he has done extensive research on these matters. The body of his viewpoint is a summary of his research, a list of short statements and statistics presented as facts, without examples or supporting arguments. How persuasive is this approach? Does Mead succeed in his opening in establishing that he could support his claims if he were given more space? How do the author's tone, the format of the bulleted lists, and the use of statistics affect his credibility?

Welfare Reform Has Not Helped People Escape Poverty

Premilla Nadasen

"Although many have left welfare, few have escaped poverty."

In the viewpoint that follows, Premilla Nadasen addresses the 2006 reauthorization of the 1996 welfare reform and contends that the reauthorization's new policies harm the people welfare is intended to help. Although reform has reduced the number of people who are supported by welfare, she argues, many of the people who have left welfare are still living in poverty. She concludes that welfare reform has taken away the help that poor families need. Nadasen is an associate professor of history at Queens College, City University of New York, and the author of *Welfare Warriors: The Welfare Rights Movement in the United States* (2004).

AS YOU READ, CONSIDER THE FOLLOWING QUESTIONS:
1. According to state administrators cited in the viewpoint, which people have not yet found jobs under the requirements of welfare reform?
2. Which type of family is most likely to be poor, according to the viewpoint?
3. What is meant by the term "food insecurity," as used in the viewpoint?

P resident [George W.] Bush . . . signed a bill making it harder for states and participants in welfare-to-work programs to get the help they need.

The bill reauthorized the 1996 welfare reform, which Congress and the [Bill] Clinton administration designed to push recipients off welfare rolls and onto employment rolls. After 2002, states were required to have at least half of the recipients working or else face a cut in funding.

But in his announcement on June 28, [2006] Health and Human Services Secretary Mike Leavitt issued stricter work guidelines. States were previously allowed to use their 1995 welfare population as a target for the percentage who were enrolled in work programs. The new regulations require states to start counting from their welfare

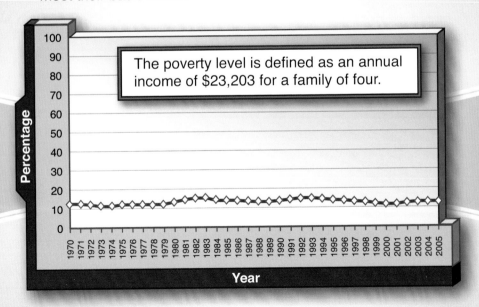

Percentage of Americans Living Below the Poverty Level, 1970–2005

Advocates for the poor have long held that the current poverty level understates the number of Americans who struggle to meet their basic needs.

The poverty level is defined as an annual income of $23,203 for a family of four.

Taken from: Public Agenda for Citizens, Issue Guide: "Poverty and Welfare." www.publicagenda.org/citizen/issueguides/poverty-and-welfare/getfacts. Source: "Income, Poverty and Health Insurance Coverage in the United States: 2005," U.S. Census Bureau, August 2006.

populations as of 2005, thus putting greater pressure on states to find work for welfare recipients who remain on the rolls.

The net effect of these stricter rules will be to push more families off welfare.

Since the Temporary Assistance [for] Needy Families (TANF) program started in 1996, the welfare population has dropped from 4 million to 1.9 million. Nearly all recipients who are capable of work have already been removed from the welfare rolls. Wisconsin, a pioneer in welfare-to-work programs, reduced its caseload by 80 percent.

State welfare administrators agree that most employable recipients have already left the welfare program. Those who are left are the poorest of the poor who have physical or emotional disabilities or substance abuse problems. They are unlikely to obtain steady employment. As a result, funding will be cut.

> **FAST FACT**
>
> The number of Americans receiving food stamps in 2008 reached 29 million, the highest level since the program began, according to the U.S. Department of Agriculture. Half of those receiving food aid are children.

The fundamental question, however, is whether former welfare recipients are actually faring any better than they were 10 years ago.

Leaving Welfare, Not Poverty

Although poverty rates fell during the economic boom of the 1990s, they have risen steadily again since 2000. Single-parent families headed by women are the hardest hit. They are two-and-a-half times more likely to be poor than two-parent families with children.

Despite the assertion by Wade F. Horn, the Health and Human Services assistant secretary for children and families, that "the only way to escape poverty is through work," this is not the reality for most low-wage workers.

[In July 2006] a full-time worker at the current federal minimum wage of $5.15 an hour earns $10,700 annually, $5,000 below the poverty line for a family of three.

According to the U.S. Department of Agriculture, 13 million children in America experience "food insecurity" and do not have access to enough healthy foods. Some resources are available, such as this food bank in Ohio.

Nearly all studies show that the number of homeless families with children has increased significantly over the past decade. According to the National Law Center on Homelessness and Poverty, in 2003, 39 percent of the homeless were children under the age of 18.

According to the U.S. Department of Agriculture, 13 million children in the United States experience "food insecurity." This means they lack consistent access to enough food for active, healthy living.

Thus, although many have left welfare, few have escaped poverty. Poor families face enormous obstacles in paying for child care, skyrocketing housing costs, health care and transportation.

The federal government's concerted efforts to shred the safety net— including the abolition of Aid to Families with Dependent Children in 1996, cuts to public education and a reduction in social service programs—have exacerbated these problems by forcing families to spread limited resources even more widely.

A more practical and fair approach would be to increase the minimum wage; help subsidize housing and child care; make health care affordable; and provide economic assistance to families in need.

Overworked parents don't have time to help children with their homework or meet with their child's teacher. They are unable to supervise minors during non-school hours or give troubled children needed attention.

As a nation, we should create opportunities—not barriers—to improving the lives of poor families.

EVALUATING THE AUTHORS' ARGUMENTS:

Both of the authors you have just read agree that one effect of welfare reform has been to reduce the number of people on welfare. Mead sees this as a good thing, because it shows that more people are supporting themselves without relying on the government. Nadasen sees it as a bad thing, because many of the people who are supporting themselves without welfare are struggling. Can both authors be right? How should a government balance the goals of providing for its citizens and supporting their independence?

Welfare Creates Dependency in Those It Serves

"Those who depended on the government . . . were left for days to the mercy of armed thugs."

Brendan Miniter

In the following viewpoint Brendan Miniter analyses what happened to poor people who were unable to evacuate New Orleans after Hurricane Katrina hit the city; he argues that it was dependence on the welfare state that held them in the city. Because people on welfare have come to expect the government to solve their problems, he contends, the New Orleans victims did not have the energy or the knowledge to save themselves. In his conclusion, the author proposes new programs to give people in poverty more responsibility for their economic decisions. Miniter is assistant editor of OpinionJournal.com, an online feature of the *Wall Street Journal.*

AS YOU READ, CONSIDER THE FOLLOWING QUESTIONS:
1. According to the liberals cited in the viewpoint, why were so many poor people left behind when New Orleans was evacuated?
2. What fraction of New Orleans residents was living below the poverty line before the hurricane, according to the viewpoint?
3. According to the author, what is the most likely path by which a poor person can reach the middle class?

"What the American people have seen [is] this incredible disparity in which those people who had cars and money got out, and those people who were impoverished died."

The above comment about Hurricane Katrina comes to us from Ted Kennedy, who went on to say that the question for [September 2005 prospective] Chief Justice John Roberts is whether he stands for "a fairer, more just nation" or will use "narrow, stingy interpretations of the law to frustrate progress." But why stop there? Sen. Kennedy is onto something and, indeed, the question isn't only for Judge Roberts. It's also one for the national debate now under way in the wake of the most devastating hurricane to hit the U.S. in decades.

That debate has so far largely focused on race and class to explain why tens of thousands of poor people were left behind to fend for themselves in a flooding city. Liberals are now blaming small-government

Some experts say that Hurricane Katrina victims in New Orleans were failed by a welfare system that made them too dependent on the government.

conservatism for cutting "antipoverty" programs. That's a tune a surprising number of people are starting to hum, from NAACP [National Association for the Advancement of Colored People] chairman Julian Bond to *New York Times* columnist David Brooks, who speculated recently that the storm will probably spark a new progressive movement in America. The lyrics are still being written, but the refrain for this ditty is a familiar one: *Small government conservatives did it to us again.*

There is, however, another explanation: The welfare state failed the residents of the Lower Ninth Ward and other flooded New Orleans neighborhoods long before the levees gave way. This gets us back to the question Sen. Kennedy wants Judge Roberts to answer about whether to adopt a narrow view that prevents real progress from taking place. And it also explains the role [New Orleans] Mayor Ray Nagin and [Louisiana] Gov. Kathleen Blanco—both Democrats—played in leaving mostly poor, minority citizens in a city that was clearly descending into chaos.

FAST FACT

In a survey conducted by the Survelum Public Data Bank, 32 percent of respondents expressed the opinion that government assistance does more harm than good. Another 26 percent disagreed, while 29 percent were not sure.

A Failing City

Anyone who has taken a non-drinking-binge tour of New Orleans, venturing outside the French Quarter and Garden District, might have noticed that New Orleans was a failing city. Tourism kept it, well, afloat, but large swaths of the city were mired in poverty for decades. One out of four New Orleans residents was living below the poverty line, and tens of thousands of people were living in public housing. These are the people who were left behind in the flood and who have long been left behind by failing schools, lack of economic opportunity, and crime well above the national average.

The Lower Ninth Ward was one section particularly hard hit by the blight of poverty. Another hit hard by both poverty and then the flood was the Sixth Ward, home of the infamous Lafitte housing

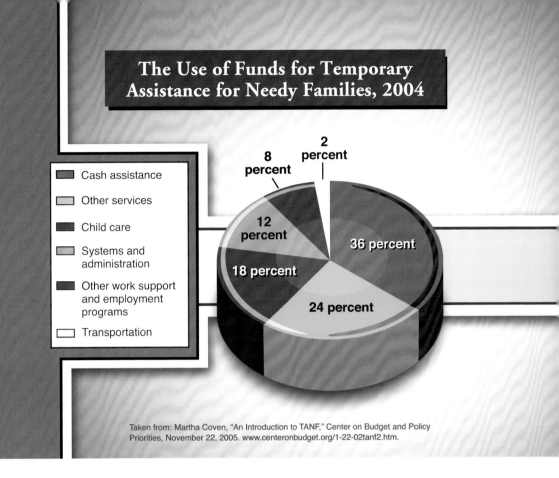

The Use of Funds for Temporary Assistance for Needy Families, 2004

- Cash assistance
- Other services
- Child care
- Systems and administration
- Other work support and employment programs
- Transportation

2 percent

8 percent

12 percent

18 percent

36 percent

24 percent

Taken from: Martha Coven, "An Introduction to TANF," Center on Budget and Policy Priorities, November 22, 2005. www.centeronbudget.org/1-22-02tanf2.htm.

project. Recently the murder of a teenager there sparked a high school class to write short, locally published books about Lafitte's horrible living conditions. One author and a Lafitte resident, Ashley Nelson, told NPR [National Public Radio] . . . that her friends and relatives still hadn't been able to escape their flooded neighborhood.

That's not to say there was a lack of funding or even a lack of interest in poverty "elimination" programs. For decades city, state and federal officials poured good money after bad into public housing and other programs. In the 1940s the Housing Authority of New Orleans built several public housing apartment buildings near the French Quarter. As the decades passed more money and more programs followed. In 1993 the Clinton administration recognized that packing public housing units into a small space didn't eliminate poverty, but it did create ghettoes that were not well served by public transportation or emergency services.

To solve the problem the Clinton administration launched the "Hope VI" housing program which called for partnerships with private developers to build "mixed income" housing. In 2001 one of the vintage 1940s public housing buildings—the St. Thomas complex—was torn down and replaced by a private development called River Gardens. It would be interesting to know how many River Gardens residents got out of the city ahead of the flood waters compared with those who lived in the remaining public housing units nearby.

Depending on the Government

We still only have anecdotal evidence to go on, and we can be hopeful as the death toll remains far below the thousands originally predicted. But it's reasonable to surmise that Sen. Kennedy is correct about those who wanted to leave: Most people who could arrange for their own transportation got out of harm's way; those who depended on the government (and public transportation) were left for days to the mercy of armed thugs at the Superdome and Convention Center. It was an extreme example of what the welfare state has done to the poor for decades: use the promise of food, shelter and other necessities to lure most of the poor to a few central points and then leave them stranded and nearly helpless.

This isn't a failure of President [George W.] Bush's compassionate conservatism. Nor is it evidence that Ronald Reagan's philosophy of smaller government is fatally flawed. If LBJ [Lyndon Baines Johnson, U.S. president from 1963 to 1969] had won his war on poverty, Ninth Ward residents would have had the means to drive themselves out of New Orleans. Instead, after decades and billions of tax dollars have been poured into big government programs, one out of four people in the Big Easy were still poor. That is an indictment of the welfare state and all its antipoverty programs.

It is time to break free of the narrow thinking that has prevented progress for decades. It's time to rethink how we, as a society, combat poverty. Are we going to try another big-government program and expect better results this time? Or are we now going to realize that ownership is the most likely path to the middle class? School vouchers can help poor parents take ownership of their children's education and finally break the grip teachers unions have on the public schools. Health savings accounts and private accounts for Medicaid and Social Security will give those on the lower rungs of the economic ladder the skills as well as the assets necessary to climb higher. In late August [2005] the levees broke in New Orleans. But the welfare state had left the poor stuck in the mud long before that.

EVALUATING THE AUTHORS' ARGUMENTS:

In the viewpoint you have just read, Brendan Miniter uses a dramatic example—the destruction caused by Hurricane Katrina—to make a point about the welfare system in general. In the next viewpoint, Richard Wolf tells the stories of several individual families. How do these examples and anecdotes affect the way you read the viewpoints? As a reader, are you more persuaded by stories or by statistics?

Viewpoint

4

Welfare Reform Has Lessened Dependency

"'You have to get out and look for a job. . . . You just can't rely on the system anymore.'"

Richard Wolf

In the following viewpoint journalist Richard Wolf tells the stories of several single mothers who have been forced by welfare reform to find jobs. Nationwide, he explains, millions of families have left the welfare system and found employment since welfare reform became law in 1996. Although many of these workers struggle to support their families with the low wages they earn, Wolf demonstrates that for many women, lessened dependence on the government has led to new skills and new confidence. Wolf is a Washington correspondent for *USA Today*.

AS YOU READ, CONSIDER THE FOLLOWING QUESTIONS:
1. According to the viewpoint, what percentage of families on welfare are headed by unmarried women?
2. As mentioned in the viewpoint, what is the time limit for receiving cash benefits from the welfare system?
3. What lessons have Michelle Gordon's children learned from her struggles, as reported in the viewpoint?

Michelle Gordon was 30, a poor, single mother with four kids between 5 and 13, when the federal government decided in 1996 that parents on welfare should go to work.

Since then, Gordon's life has been "a little bit of a roller coaster." She has held about 10 jobs—at a call center, as a nurse's aide, as a janitorial supervisor, most recently at a grocery store. She lost that job on April 19 [2006], her 40th birthday. It took her two months to find another. For 25 hours a week, she cleans bathrooms and vacuums floors at a drug rehabilitation center.

Mary Bradford was 45 in 1996, with three children between 11 and 25, when she traded welfare for a job filling orders at Victorian Trading Co. Ten years later, her office has moved from Missouri to Kansas, and she's still with the company. She's a production supervisor, and her earnings have more than doubled from the $7 an hour she made in 1996. "Most likely, I'll retire from here," Bradford says.

"She's reliable as the sun coming up," says Randy Rolston, the company's co-founder. "I can't think of a day she's missed."

The paths that Gordon and Bradford have traveled illustrate the successes and frustrations in the decade since the nation's welfare system was overhauled to require work and limit benefits.

A Philosophical Shift

The law signed by President [Bill] Clinton on Aug. 22, 1996, has transformed the way the nation helps its neediest citizens. Gone is the promise of a government check for parents raising children in poverty. In its place are 50 state programs to help those parents get jobs.

In the . . . years since caseloads peaked at 5.1 million families in 1994, millions have left the welfare rolls for low-paying jobs. Nearly

> # FAST FACT
>
> The federal government defines people as "dependent" on welfare if they receive more than half of their income from Temporary Assistance for Needy Families (TANF), food stamps, and Supplemental Security Income (SSI). According to the U.S. Department of Health and Human Services, 3 million fewer Americans were dependent on welfare in 2004 than in 1996.

Welfare Recipients' Average Monthly Benefits

The value of the average monthly payment to recipients of aid through the former Aid to Families with Dependent Children (AFDC) or the current Temporary Assistance for Needy Families (TANF) has declined, forcing families to find other means of supporting themselves.

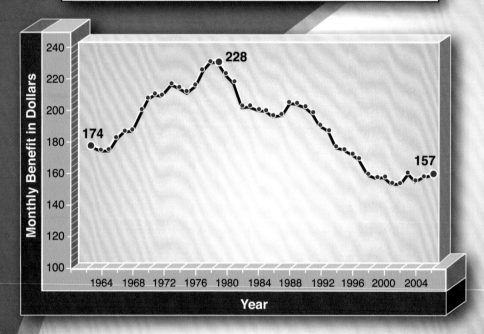

Taken from: U.S. Department of Health and Human Services, Annual Report to Congress: Indicators of Welfare Dependence, 2007. http://aspehhs.gov/hsp/indicators07/apa.pdf.

1 million more have been kicked off for not following states' rules or have used up all the benefits they're allowed under time limits. Today, 1.9 million families get cash benefits; in one-third of them, only the children qualify for aid. About 38% of those still on welfare are black, 33% white and 24% Hispanic.

Three in four families on welfare are headed by unmarried women. As a result, employment rates for all single women rose 25% before declining slightly since 2001. Earnings for the poorest 40% of families headed by women doubled from 1994 to 2000, before recession wiped out nearly half the gains. Poverty rates for children fell 25% before rising 10% since 2000.

"It was a profoundly important philosophic shift," says Health and Human Services (HHS) Secretary Michael Leavitt, who was governor of Utah when the law was implemented. "This was . . . one of the few things in a decade you can look at and say the world really changed."

Many welfare experts, however, cite continuing problems. Liberals such as Olivia Golden of the Urban Institute, who ran the nation's welfare program in 1996, say more government services such as child care assistance are needed to help single parents succeed in the workplace. Conservatives such as Robert Rector of the Heritage Foundation say states should be forcing more of those who remain on welfare to prepare for work. Ron Haskins of the Brookings Institution, who helped write the new law when he worked for Congress, worries that too many women on welfare have turned into the working poor.

Gordon typifies that concern. Between her many jobs, she used up her cash benefits under the five-year time limit imposed by the welfare overhaul. Without work, she lost her federal housing subsidy, which helped pay her rent. So in October [2005], she and three of her kids moved in with her mother. Her oldest son is in jail; she cares for his

In the United States three out of four families on welfare are headed by women.

6-year-old daughter. The three fathers of her children pay no child support. She gets about $500 a month in food stamps.

These days, the family mows lawns to help make ends meet. "Things are really rough out here," Gordon says. "We do what we need to do to have money." . . .

Welfare-to-Work Success

Parents who have left welfare are spread throughout . . . the nation. Some are succeeding. Others are struggling.

At the local welfare office, workers Carol Ward and Charlese Henderson are thriving. Ward, 52, got a high school equivalency diploma, job training and child care through the welfare-to-work program. Now she's a clerical aide earning about $17,000 a year. "This job saved me," she says.

Henderson, 31, who had the first of her four children at 14, is a $26,000-a-year caseworker after running through about a dozen lesser jobs over the past 15 years. She has little sympathy for clients who aren't motivated to work. "I had a co-worker tell me that I'm not very compassionate," she says.

At home and out of work, Patricia Williams is struggling. She needs a few months of cash benefits to get through the summer, until her part-time job in the kitchen of a charter high school resumes. Welfare officials say she's used up 54 of her 60 months under the law. "You have to get out and look for a job," Williams, 43, says. "You just can't rely on the system anymore."

At a local business and technology community college, Sandy Carson and Gary Trimble are somewhere in between. They are getting nearly a year's training for jobs in manufacturing. Trimble, 50, a self-employed carpenter who cares for his 16-year-old son, wound up on welfare after a seven-month jail term for a child-support violation. "I really felt lost," he says. "I went in telling them right out of the gate, 'I want school.'"

Carson, 42, left her postal clerk's job seven years ago to care for a son, then 3, with a disability. She wants to work with animals, but she considers herself lucky to be in the manufacturing course. "It's not my dream job, but it's something I can do," she says.

For Michelle Gordon, making ends meet these days depends on two lawn mowers, two trimmers and a broom. "I'm living with my mother. I'm 40 years old," she says.

The Hope for Future Generations

She uses her experience as a lesson to her children. Daughter Essence, 19, has a high school diploma and a job and is attending college. Son Geno, 17, also has a summer job. Daughter Zoila, 15, says she won't have kids until she's married and established in life. The family gets food stamps, and the youngest two are on Medicaid, but they no longer get cash benefits.

The roller coaster Gordon has been riding for 10 years has made her less dependent on the government and more of a role model for her kids, she says.

"I'm not making $50,000 a year," she says, "but I'm keeping my head up, and I'm surviving."

> **EVALUATING THE AUTHOR'S ARGUMENTS:**
>
> The viewpoint you have just read is one of only a small number of viewpoints in this volume that includes quotations from people on welfare. How do these quotations affect the way you respond to the people described in the viewpoint? Why might Richard Wolf think it is important to include the voices of welfare recipients, who are likely to have a strong bias, as well as those of supposedly objective government experts?

Marriage Promotion Rules Have Strengthened Families

Wade F. Horn

"What separates stable and healthy marriages from unstable and unhealthy ones is not the frequency of conflict, but how couples manage conflict."

In the following viewpoint Wade F. Horn argues that the Healthy Marriage Initiative, created under President George W. Bush, will help children escape poverty by helping their parents marry and form strong families. Children do best when they live with their married parents, he argues, and couples with access to marriage education stand the best chance of staying married. By encouraging healthy marriages, he concludes, the government will eventually be able to reduce expensive programs that serve poor children. When he wrote this viewpoint, Horn was the assistant secretary for children and families at the U.S. Department of Health and Human Services, a position he held from 2001 to 2007.

AS YOU READ, CONSIDER THE FOLLOWING QUESTIONS:
1. According to the viewpoint, would couples be required to participate in marriage education under the Healthy Marriage Initiative?
2. Why, according to the viewpoint, does the Healthy Marriage Initiative target mainly low-income families?
3. As reported by the author, how much does the Administration for Children and Families spend each year?

The . . . report from the National Marriage Project at Rutgers University—"The State of Our Unions, 2005"—is the latest in a series of such reports to document our cultural retreat from marriage. Although divorce rates have declined from all-time highs in the early 1980s, more men and women are cohabiting—many of them with children—rather than marrying.

This is not good news; at least not for children. That's because research consistently finds that cohabiting relationships are far more unstable than marriage. Wherever one finds family instability, an increased risk of problems for children follows with all the associated impacts on social institutions and the demand for more (and more expensive) governmental interventions.

In contrast, healthy and stable marriages support children and limit the need for government programs. Whether the problem is abuse, neglect, or poverty, research clearly shows the best chance a child has of avoiding these problems is to grow up with their mom and dad in a stable, healthy marriage.

Marriages Are Worth Preserving

In the face of these trends, some counsel resignation. High divorce rates and increasing cohabitation rates are simply a reflection of modernity, they say, and besides, there is not much anyone can do about it.

We disagree. Armed with compelling research that shows that children do best when reared in healthy, stable, two-parent households, [in 2002] President [George W.] Bush launched his Healthy Marriage Initiative. The initiative's goal is to help couples who choose marriage for themselves gain greater access, on a voluntary

The Healthy Marriage Initiative provided more than $1.5 billion for training, as in this class in Pennsylvania, to help couples develop skills to sustain healthy marriages.

basis, to services where they can develop the skills and knowledge necessary to form and sustain a healthy marriage. The initiative is based on solid research indicating that what separates stable and healthy marriages from unstable and unhealthy ones is not the frequency of conflict, but how couples manage conflict. The good news is that through marriage education, healthy conflict-resolution skills can be taught.

The president's Healthy Marriage Initiative is a centerpiece of welfare-reform reauthorization bills [placed in 2005] before both houses of Congress. The reason why the president's Healthy Marriage Initiative mainly targets low-income couples is not because we believe marriage is particularly problematic in low-income communities, but because unlike more affluent couples, low-income couples either do not have the resources to purchase marriage-education services or those services are not currently available in their community. The aim, then, of the president's Healthy Marriage Initiative is to give low-income couples greater access to marriage-education services and thereby improve their chances of forming healthy, stable marriages.

Promoting Limited Government?

But, some libertarians and fiscal conservatives worry, is this initiative really consistent with a conservative's view of limited government? Good question. Here's our answer: First, the president's Healthy Marriage Initiative does not add a penny to the federal budget. Rather, our plan simply redirects money from two existing incentive funds under the Temporary Assistance for Needy Families (TANF) program, incentive funds which most impartial observers agree have not been particularly effective.

Second, rather than an expansion of government, the president's Healthy Marriage Initiative is an exercise in *limited government.* Here's how: I run the Administration for Children and Families at the U.S. Department of Health and Human Services. My agency spends $46 billion per year operating 65 different social programs. If one goes down the list of these programs—from child welfare, to child-support enforcement, to anti-poverty assistance to runaway-youth initiatives—the need for each is either created or exacerbated by the breakup of families and marriages. It doesn't take a PhD to understand that controlling the growth of these programs depends on preventing problems from happening in the first place. One way to accomplish that—not the only way, of course, but one way—is to help couples form and sustain healthy marriages.

Indeed, government is most intrusive into family life when marriages fail. If you don't believe it, try getting married, having kids

> **FAST FACT**
>
> Several states have their own programs to promote marriage as a way to get low-income women off welfare. For example, West Virginia gives poor married couples one hundred dollars a month more in their welfare checks than unmarried recipients receive.

and then getting a divorce. If you are a non-custodial parent, government will tell you when you can see your children; whether you can pick them up after school or not, and if so, on what days; whether you

The number of households with children younger than fifteen, headed by unmarried couples, rose between 1960 and 2000.

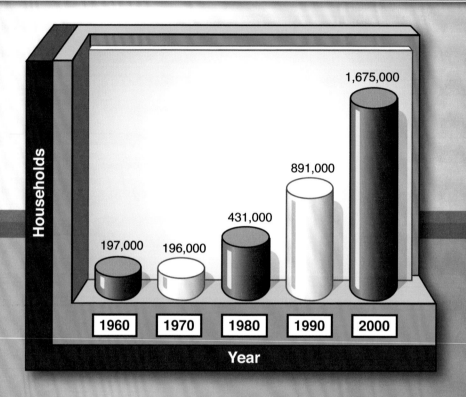

Households

1,675,000

891,000

431,000

197,000 196,000

1960 1970 1980 1990 2000

Year

Taken from: "NRFC Quick Statistics: Fathers and Cohabitation," National Responsible Fatherhood Clearinghouse, U.S. Department of Health and Human Services, 2002. www.fatherhood.gov/documents/qs_cohabitation.pdf.

can authorize medical care for your children; and how much money you must spend on your kids. By preventing marital breakup in the first place—not by making divorce harder to get, but by increasing the odds of a stable marriage by increasing marital health and happiness—one obviates the need for such intrusive government.

The good news is that welfare reform has been a tremendous success. A pernicious culture of dependency was transformed into one that is now focused on helping those on welfare obtain and maintain employment. As a result, welfare rolls have decreased by 60 percent since 1960; earnings by single-parent-headed households are at an all-time high; and child poverty has declined significantly, particularly for African-American and Hispanic children.

The job, however, is not done. One of the main goals of welfare reform is to increase the proportion of children growing up in two-parent married households. The president's Healthy Marriage Initiative, by offering voluntary marriage-education services to those who can't afford them, will strengthen marriage and prevent expensive, painful and oftentimes intractable social problems for children. It's a common-sense ounce of prevention that will help temper the demand for a pound of costly social interventions later.

EVALUATING THE AUTHOR'S ARGUMENTS:

In the viewpoint you have just read, Wade F. Horn argues that helping couples marry and stay married is an appropriate goal of the federal government, because it protects children and saves money in the long run. Do you agree? What factors should be considered when a community determines which matters are private, and which matters are in the public interest?

Marriage Promotion Rules Address the Wrong Problems

Jean Hardisty

"[Environmental] burdens make it difficult to set up stable, economically viable households, and also put stresses on couples that do marry."

In the following viewpoint Jean Hardisty argues that government plans to encourage low-income couples to marry will not relieve poverty. There are many reasons single mothers do not marry their children's fathers, she contends, and many of those reasons are sound, or beyond the government's control. Hardisty concludes that if the government truly wants to help women escape poverty, it should support education and employment programs rather than encouraging marriage. Hardisty is a senior scholar at the Wellesley Centers for Women, and the author of *Marriage as a Cure for Poverty: A Bogus Formula for Women*.

AS YOU READ, CONSIDER THE FOLLOWING QUESTIONS:

1. Under the terms of the 2005 Deficit Reduction Act, how much will be spent over five years to promote marriage, according to the viewpoint?

Jean Hardisty, "Promoting Marriage to Cure Poverty?" *Peacework*, April 1, 2007. Reproduced by permission of the author.

2. What are some of the reasons that middle-class and professional women with children are unmarried, as reported in the viewpoint?
3. According to researchers mentioned in the viewpoint, what are the two most important predictors that a person will escape poverty?

Flying well under the radar of public consciousness, the 2005 Deficit Reduction Act authorized $100 million for the promotion of marriage for low-income women and an additional $50 million to support fatherhood initiatives for low-income couples. The authorization extends for five years, with a total allocation of $750 million. At the same time, Congress reauthorized the Personal Responsibility and Work Opportunity Reconciliation Act (PRWORA), originally passed in 1996 under [President Bill] Clinton.

The current [President George W. Bush] Administration has been funding marriage promotion for at least five years, primarily through the Department of Health and Human Services. Most of this funding (in excess of $20 million) has been directed to programs for low-income women, especially those who are receiving welfare.

Taxpayers might assume that the program is driven by solid evidence from the social sciences that marriage does indeed result in a higher income for poor women. But *there is no such evidence.* This is a program driven by right wing ideology and a backlash against the social reforms of the 1970s and 1980s. . . .

Marriage in the United States

There is undoubtedly a link between single motherhood and poverty, and it is therefore likely true that an increase in single motherhood is a major factor in increased child poverty. But a growing body of literature that examines the increase in single motherhood among middle-class and professional women—due to divorce, parenthood in a lesbian couple where the mother is usually counted as "single," or the decision to bear children without a partner—calls into question the assertion that single motherhood is itself what leads to poverty. These middle-class mothers tend not to experience poverty as the

President George W. Bush signs the Deficit Reduction Act in 2005. Opponents of the bill say the act was a backlash against the social reforms of the 1970s.

result of bearing or adopting children. They may be attacked by the Religious Right for their "selfishness" in deciding to raise a child without a father present, but they are often praised by sociologists as women who have taken charge of their lives and are courageously exercising their own agency.

However, single mothers who are low-income, especially those receiving welfare benefits, are constantly criticized by the general public, and are held accountable for their single status rather than praised for finding self-fulfillment in motherhood. They are usually judged to be irresponsible, or simply unable to meet the child's needs, including the supposed need for a father or father figure.

By examining the scant research that has actually asked welfare recipients what they would like in their lives, we learn that a large percentage of single low-income mothers would like to be married at some time. They seek marriages that are financially stable, with a loving, supportive husband who has no addictions and does not threaten their children. Welfare recipients, like many other U.S. women, often aspire to a romantic notion of marriage and family that features a white picket fence in the suburbs. According to the proponents of "marriage promotion" programs, women and men just need a little nudge to encourage them to take the step that will lead in the direction of that picket fence—to marry and stay married.

But very often, a low-income woman's life experience teaches her another lesson. Many low-income women see their children as their greatest accomplishment (as do many mothers of all classes) and are clear that their job is to take care of them. That means providing a safe environment and "being there" for them. Contrary to the characteristic middle-class view of teenage childbirth as the curtailment of a young woman's chances for success, low-income mothers often credit their early motherhood with keeping them away from a life of drugs, or crime, or violence. Marriage is a goal, but financial stability and the children come first.

Barriers to Marriage

Most researchers agree that in the minds of the white public, a welfare recipient is an African American woman, though to date Blacks have never been the majority of welfare recipients. The slander and demonization of women of color, especially African American women, so characteristic of discussions of welfare, are part and parcel of the structural racism that pervades U.S. society.

FAST FACT

According to the National Responsible Fatherhood Clearinghouse, more than two-thirds of poor, unmarried parents agree that a single parent can raise a child as well as a married couple.

Race accounts for several barriers to marriage in low-income communities of color. The disparate incarceration of men of color, job discrimination, and police harassment are three barriers that are race-specific. Other barriers are universally present for low-income people: low-quality and unsafe housing, a decrepit and underfunded educational system; joblessness; poor health care; and flat-funded day care for six consecutive years are some of the challenges faced by low-income women and men. These burdens make it difficult to set up stable, economically viable households, and also put stresses on couples that do marry.

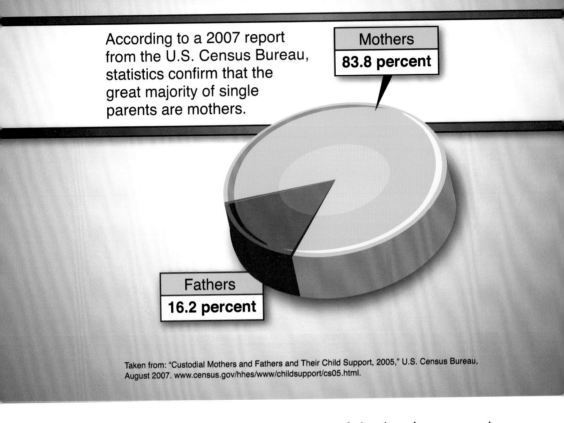

Gender Diversity in Single Parents, 2007

According to a 2007 report from the U.S. Census Bureau, statistics confirm that the great majority of single parents are mothers.

Mothers
83.8 percent

Fathers
16.2 percent

Taken from: "Custodial Mothers and Fathers and Their Child Support, 2005," U.S. Census Bureau, August 2007. www.census.gov/hhes/www/childsupport/cs05.html.

But it is not these barriers that current federal and state marriage programs address. Most programs favored by the Bush Administration focus on developing relationship skills and encouraging the mother and father of a newborn to marry. Some of the programs to improve a woman's relationship with her partner, such as those of The Gottman Institute, are respected within the field of psychology and do not contain a religious component. But far too many, such as Marriage Savers and the Northwest Marriage Institute, are Biblically-based or driven by rightist ideology about gender roles within the family which should disqualify them as providers of neutral counseling for couples. It is currently impossible to monitor all the opportunities for those receiving federal and state money to pressure welfare recipients in ways that make them feel threatened if they do not participate in a marriage promotion program.

There is widespread agreement among researchers that the two greatest predictors to leaving poverty are education and a good job. Yet the 2005 Deficit Reduction Act cut the funding available for welfare recipients to participate in education and Congress refused to raise the minimum wage for six years until 2007. It is clear that, in the fight to end poverty, ideology often trumps facts.

EVALUATING THE AUTHORS' ARGUMENTS:

In the two viewpoints you have just read, the authors both base their arguments on research. Horn states that "research consistently finds" that marriage is more stable than cohabitation; Hardisty refers to a "growing body of research" that questions the connection between single mothers and poverty. Can both authors be right? When opposing authors both claim that the research supports their positions, how can a general reader—who may not have access to the research, or the ability to understand it—decide whom to believe?

Chapter 3

Are There Good Alternatives to Welfare?

Some experts say that charitable organizations such as the Salvation Army are better equipped than the government to aid people struggling to meet their basic needs.

Private Charities Can Successfully Serve the Poor

"Those organizations that work directly with poor people stand a better chance of learning how to meet their needs."

Arnold Kling

In the following viewpoint libertarian economist Arnold Kling contends that government does not do a good job of helping poor people because government programs are shaped by special interests rather than by necessity. Charitable organizations, he argues, are more flexible, more accountable, and more efficient. He proposes that the poor would be better served by a new tax policy that directs more money to private charities and less to the government. Kling is a scholar with the Cato Institute, a nonprofit public policy research foundation, and a contributing editor of TCS Daily, an online journal that examines current issues, including law and politics, where this viewpoint first appeared.

AS YOU READ, CONSIDER THE FOLLOWING QUESTIONS:

1. According to the author, which government assistance program seems to have been a success?
2. What can charities demand in exchange for their help, according to the viewpoint?
3. Under the terms of the author's plan described in the viewpoint, how would a charitable donation affect the donor's taxes?

Arnold Kling, "Libertarianism and Poverty," TCSdaily.com, June 5, 2006. Reproduced by permission.

This essay outlines a libertarian approach to poverty. No, it's not "Leave them in the gutter." It's an approach that tries to be pragmatic and compassionate. Even if—especially if—you are not a libertarian, you need to understand that when it comes to government doing something about poverty, "less is more." Further, below, I even include a policy proposal—something that is rare coming from a libertarian.

I describe myself as a pragmatic libertarian. If I had to give up a little bit of freedom in order to see a meaningful reduction in poverty, I would do so. My problem with government is that I see it doing harm on both counts. . . .

The Government Record

Government has a mixed record in alleviating poverty. The GI bill [a government package of benefits for military veterans] seems to me to have been a success. Welfare seems to have been a failure—by creating a culture of entitlement for unwed mothers, it exacerbated the very problem that it was supposed to cure. Social Security probably was a positive program when it began, but by now I believe it causes too much hardship for people of working age relative to the hardship that it relieves for the retired, and this tendency is going to get worse with each passing decade. . . .

Government programs persist not because they help to alleviate social problems but because they develop political constituencies. Thus, we have a food stamp program, when the number one nutritional problem among the poor appears to be obesity. I am not saying that I don't think that poor people need help obtaining food. But a program that was focused on poor people rather than as an indirect way to aid the farming constituency would probably operate rather differently than our existing food stamp program. With government, political goals inevitably interfere with what from an idealistic perspective would be the "public good" intent of a program.

Of course, one can support government programs in spite of the inevitable political dysfunction. Just because it is not perfect does not mean that it is wrong. But I believe that we can do better with less government and more decentralized programs to address poverty. . . .

The Role of Charitable Organizations

Charitable organizations are better than government as a source of aid. First, it is easier for donors to hold charitable organizations accountable than it is for taxpayers to hold government accountable. A failed government program can go on forever. An ineffective charity has a more difficult time obtaining funding.

Sources of Revenue for Public Charities, 2005

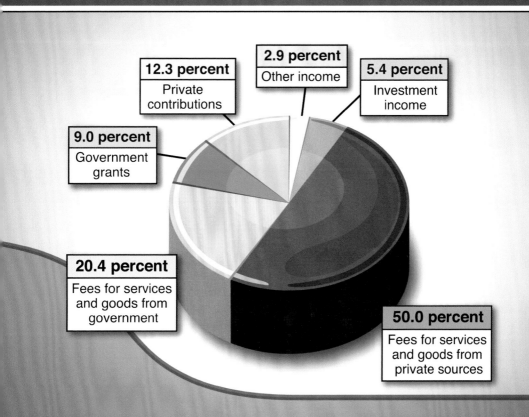

12.3 percent
Private contributions

2.9 percent
Other income

5.4 percent
Investment income

9.0 percent
Government grants

20.4 percent
Fees for services and goods from government

50.0 percent
Fees for services and goods from private sources

Charitable organizations tend to be more "hands-on" with the needy than are government organizations. For example, although I cannot say that I am particularly happy that my daughter volunteered to go on a project with [a particular] organization, it clearly is going to put her in direct contact with poor people, which is better than going on an international "mission" where you stay in 4-star hotels.

Those organizations that work directly with poor people stand a better chance of learning how to meet their needs than people who lobby in Washington on behalf of the poor. Nongovernmental organizations [NGO's] will tend to be more innovative. They can be leaner, and they can operate with what the military would call a high "tooth to tail" ratio.

Charitable organizations are better suited to dealing with the pathology of poverty. When people get checks from the government, they tend to think of this as an entitlement. They are getting money in exchange for doing nothing. They learn that this is how you get money—you take it from others. Taking money from others is what criminals do. Productive people get money from other people by exchanging something of value.

Charities are in a position to demand something of value from their clients, even if that "something" is nothing more than a human "Thank you." Charities are also in a position to set the terms under which their clients receive aid and to cut off clients who fail to comply with those terms.

Charities can be flexible in how they handle individuals. One person may need transportation to a job. Another person may need drug rehabilitation. With hands-on involvement and with flexibility, charitable organizations are more likely to discover solutions to the pathologies of poverty.

Charitable organizations are flawed, to be sure. On average, I think that profitable companies are better managed than nonprofits. But every organization has its flaws, and charitable organizations are less flawed than government alternatives.

In fact, I think that one of the factors that inhibits the effectiveness of NGO's is that many of them are dependent on government grants for support. This forces the NGO to put much of its effort into satisfying the bureaucrats who provide the funding. That requires resources and skill sets that have nothing to do with solving the problems of people in need.

A Charitable Exemption?

Under our current tax system, donations to charity are a deduction from income. If your tax bracket is 25 percent and you give $1000 to charity, then this reduces your tax bill by $250, so that the donation only costs you $750 after taxes.

My proposal (which I suspect is not original) is that, on top of the current deduction for charitable contributions, we create a large charitable exemption, of, say $20,000. That would mean that you could donate up to $20,000 and have that amount taken off your *taxes*. Thus, the after-tax cost of your donation would be zero. For people whose annual tax obligation is less than $20,000, the income tax would essentially be optional. You could pay your taxes, or you could give an equivalent amount to charity.

A charitable exemption would have the effect of shifting resources from government to private charities. I believe that would be a net plus for people in need.

A charitable exemption would increase the proportion of money going to NGO's that comes from private donors rather than government.

The viewpoint's author argues for a new tax policy that would allow donations to charity to qualify as income tax exemptions, thus encouraging charitable giving.

I think that the effect of this would be to reward NGO's more for effectiveness and less for their ability to work the system to obtain government funding.

In his book *Good and Plenty*, Tyler Cowen argues that tax-incented charitable gift-giving has been good for the arts in America, because support for the arts has been decentralized. The idea of the charitable exemption is to mobilize those sorts of decentralized solutions to address other needs.

In theory, people could give their charitable donations to organizations that do not serve the needy. For example, people might give money to elite private universities, which already have enormous endowments and mostly serve affluent students. I would be disappointed if that were the outcome, but it would not necessarily be a worse use of money than the average government spending program.

This was once a country in which [nineteenth-century French political historian] Alexis de Tocqueville marveled at the spirit with which voluntary associations emerged to solve problems. A libertarian approach to poverty would seek to rekindle that spirit, rather than expand a government that sucks the oxygen out of families, private charities, and the very poor that it purports to help.

EVALUATING THE AUTHOR'S ARGUMENTS:

The author of the viewpoint you have just read, Arnold Kling, is a libertarian, which means he believes that people should have as much individual freedom as possible, without the interference of government. He wrote this essay for a magazine that is read primarily by people who share his views. How effective is his argument in this viewpoint that government has not done a good job of helping poor people? How might he have made his case differently if he were addressing a group that did not already agree that big government was undesirable?

Private Charities Fail to Serve Many of the Poor

"Underserved populations are not spread uniformly across the country. Neither are nonprofits."

Elizabeth T. Boris

In the following viewpoint political scientist Elizabeth T. Boris argues that government can do a more thorough job of serving poor people than charities can. Although much is not known, she contends that the existing evidence suggests that many people in need are unintentionally left out of charitable programs because these programs tend to serve the people in the immediate area or the people who belong to certain groups. Only large national charities or large government programs, she points out, have the ability to reach all segments of the population. Boris is the director for the Center on Nonprofits and Philanthropy of the Urban Institute.

AS YOU READ, CONSIDER THE FOLLOWING QUESTIONS:

1. How many nonprofit organizations have been granted tax-exempt status in the United States, as reported in the viewpoint?
2. According to the viewpoint, what percentage of Americans live below the poverty level?
3. How did the state of Arizona encourage people to give to charities that serve low-income populations, according to the viewpoint?

Elizabeth T. Boris, "Testimony of Elizabeth T. Boris, PhD, Director, Center on Nonprofits and Philanthropy The Urban Institute," U.S. House of Representatives Ways and Means Subcommittee on Oversight, September 25, 2007. Reproduced by permission.

A unique civic culture exists in the United States. It evolved through the efforts of our diverse populations reaching back before the creation of this country and it continues to evolve with every new generation and immigrant group. In our culture, we expect individuals to contribute to their communities over and above their taxes and we honor people who give and volunteer to solve problems and improve conditions in their communities, in the larger society, and throughout the world. U.S. laws recognize the value of these contributions and exempt from taxes the 1.4 million nonprofit organizations that serve public purposes, and provide tax incentives to encourage giving to a subset of almost 900,000 charitable organizations that serve the public through educational, religious, scientific, literary, poverty relief, and other activities for public benefit. . . .

Charities' Beneficiaries

Organizations are required to describe on their IRS [Internal Revenue Service] Forms 990 the accomplishments of their four largest programs, but they are not required to describe the people they serve. For some organizations, like colleges and universities, such reporting is likely to be quite easy because most track their students by multiple factors. For other types of organizations, it might be difficult to categorize the recipients of services. A soup kitchen may, by definition, serve the poor, but if it does not collect information from those it serves, it is not likely to know the ethnic, immigrant, disabled, gender, aged, or ex-offender status of that population. Collecting such information would require staff and or volunteers to gather the information, develop databases, input data, and generate reports and statistics. These steps might be difficult for small organizations, but not for larger charities with developed administrative infrastructures.

An Urban Institute study, *Nonprofit Governance in the United States: Findings from the First National Representative Study* by Francie Ostrower (2007), provides a rigorous and detailed analysis of nonprofit governance practices in the United States based on a stratified random survey of over 5,100 charities required to file the IRS Form 990. The survey asks questions about diversity of board members and of the people the organizations served. While early study reports do not focus on diversity issues, further analysis will do so. Preliminary

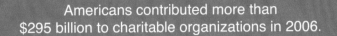

2006 Contributions by Type of Recipient Organization

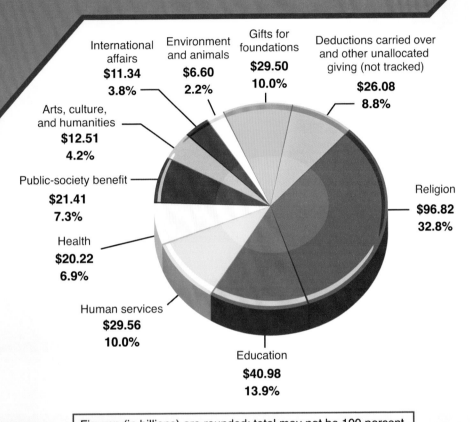

Americans contributed more than $295 billion to charitable organizations in 2006.

International affairs
$11.34
3.8%

Environment and animals
$6.60
2.2%

Gifts for foundations
$29.50
10.0%

Deductions carried over and other unallocated giving (not tracked)
$26.08
8.8%

Arts, culture, and humanities
$12.51
4.2%

Public-society benefit
$21.41
7.3%

Health
$20.22
6.9%

Human services
$29.56
10.0%

Education
$40.98
13.9%

Religion
$96.82
32.8%

Figures (in billions) are rounded; total may not be 100 percent.

Taken from: GivingUSA 2007.

results suggest that over 90 percent of nonprofits serve at least some low-income (below the poverty level) clients and that for a quarter of nonprofits, their low-income clients range between 75 and 100 percent of those they serve.

With regard to diversity, 70 percent of nonprofits have clients that are half or more white; 15 percent of nonprofits do not have any black (non-Hispanic) clients, and 3 percent serve 75 percent or more; 35 percent do not serve any Asians, and 0.9 percent serve

75 percent or more; 21 percent do not serve any Hispanic/Latino people and almost 2 percent serve 75 percent or more. For white (non-Hispanic) clients, 3 percent serve no whites, and 40 percent serve between 75 and 100 percent white clients. These preliminary findings indicate that while 40 percent of nonprofits focus on economically disadvantaged (half or more of their clients), few nonprofits serve that proportion of ethnic and racial populations.

To put the findings in context, about 13 percent of Americans live below the poverty level, but the proportion of various ethnic groups who live in poverty varies greatly. Almost 9 million of American blacks (25 percent) live in poverty, compared with almost 18 million (9 percent) of whites, over 9 million (21.5 percent) of Hispanics, and . . . 1.4 million (10.7 percent) [of Asians]. These demographics and the differences by state and regions have an impact on those served by nonprofits that have not been sufficiently analyzed.

Underserved populations are not spread uniformly across the country. Neither are nonprofits. While nationally there are approximately 10.9 nonprofits per 10,000 people, the density varies by state and region. The states with highest density of nonprofits are Vermont with 26.9 organizations per 10,000 people, Alaska with 20, and Montana with 19.2—compared with low-density states, Nevada with 5.9, and Mississippi with 6.7. Among the most populous states, Texas had 8.3 nonprofits per 10,000 people; California, 10.4; and New York, 12.5. Rural states in the upper Midwest have a denser nonprofit infrastructure than Southern states. These findings underline the potential mismatch between nonprofit resources and populations, particularly in the South. Research has not addressed the reasons for the mismatch or strategies for addressing the gaps. . . .

Gaps Between Needs and Services

There are undoubtedly gaps between needs and services, especially for the poor. Charities are largely funded by government when they provide basic human services. The makeup and needs of populations at risk are not uniform throughout the country, and government resources and priorities differ. Contracts with charities to provide welfare-type services often do not reimburse the full cost of services or provide overhead as they do for business contracts, with the result that charities must spend their resources raising money from other sources, often forgoing infrastructure improvements that would make them more efficient.

Part of the difficulty is that most giving is local, and communities differ in their makeup and needs. It is far more likely that a branch of a local youth group in Marshall Heights, or Bailey's Crossroads, Virginia, will serve Latino youth, than a branch in Potomac, Maryland, or Anacostia [in Washington, D.C.]. National nonprofits with local affiliates can often help to cross-subsidize efforts from one locality to the next, but there are issues of donor intent that may limit their ability to

Some experts contend that only the government and large charitable organizations, like the Salvation Army, have the resources to reach out to all segments of the population.

take revenues from one area to serve another. Rather, nonprofits must raise additional revenues to serve low-income populations.

Governments sometimes provide incentives for individuals to direct their contributions to organizations serving low-income populations. In Arizona, the state government implemented a special tax credit for those who give to charities that certify that more than half of those they serve are below the poverty line. This strategy has raised additional resources, but mostly for large, well-known organizations.

Immigrants are creating organizations to meet their needs. Often these come out of religious entities. In a study we are conducting of immigrant serving organizations, we identified several hundred organizations, most created in the past 15 years, that serve Latino, Asian, African, and Middle Eastern immigrants in the [Washington] D.C. metro area alone. New immigrant groups seem to be following the time-honored pattern of setting up organizations for a variety of purposes. Those include religious worship and services, human services, cultural activities, education, language instruction, and many more. Among the Latino organizations, revenue is roughly equally derived from government, contributions, and fees, but over half of the organizations do not receive government revenues. As immigrant communities move to the suburbs, they are causing a rethinking about the location of groups that serve them. There is a newly emerging dimension of civil society beginning to flourish in our immigrant communities. These new organizations may require mentoring, seed funding, and capacity building as they learn the ropes.

EVALUATING THE AUTHOR'S ARGUMENTS:

Although Elizabeth T. Boris ultimately argues that charitable giving cannot do the full job of helping low-income people, she begins her viewpoint with dramatic language describing the tradition of charity in the United States. Why do you think she begins this way? How does this passage affect your reading of the viewpoint?

The Federal Government Should Raise the Minimum Wage

"The increase . . . will allow these low-wage workers to make a little better life for themselves and their families."

Sheila Jackson Lee

The following viewpoint was originally presented by Representative Sheila Jackson Lee as a floor speech before the U.S. House of Representatives, as Congress debated H.R. 2, the Fair Minimum Wage Act of 2007. Lee argues that the federally mandated minimum wage should be increased, because many hardworking families are struggling and because the value of the minimum wage has not kept pace with inflation. The increase would benefit families, particularly women and members of minority groups, she concludes, and would help low-wage workers escape poverty. Lee, a Democrat representing the Eighteenth Congressional District of Texas, is a founder and cochair of the Congressional Children's Caucus.

Representative Sheila Jackson Lee, Floor Speech [revised and extended], U.S. House of Representatives, *Congressional Record,* January 10, 2007.

There is a biblical story about the children of Israel in the desert seeking the promised land for 40 years. . . . There are American workers who are deserving and in need of an increase in the minimum wage, and we know that for 51 years we have had the lowest valued minimum wage in America. It is clear that the minimum wage increase would help reverse the trend of declining real wages for low-wage workers, American workers, and that, between 1979 and 1989, the minimum wage lost 31 percent of its real value. . . .

FAST FACT

The federal minimum wage increased to $5.85 an hour on July 24, 2007, and to $6.55 on July 24, 2008. The Fair Minimum Wage Act of 2007, which passed with ninety-four votes to three, provides a third increase, to $7.25 an hour, on July 24, 2009.

What about the waitress who stopped me in a restaurant and said, When are you going to raise the minimum wage? A woman raising children who, with the minimum wage, will be able to have an opportunity to get a car loan to get a car to get her children to school or to the doctor or to be able to do the things that we in America enjoy doing, being with our family, providing them an opportunity?

This is a moral issue. I ask my colleagues to support the increase in the minimum wage for Americans across America. . . .

Since 2000 the cost of college tuition has risen 57 percent, which is only slightly less than the increase in the cost of gasoline. Health insurance premiums have skyrocketed by 73 percent and inflation is up 13.4 percent. But during that time, the minimum wage has not increased one cent. That is unconscionable and downright un-American. Happily, the Fair Minimum Wage Act, H.R. 2, will change this sorry state of affairs.

Today more than ever America's hard-working families are feeling squeezed, living paycheck to paycheck. I can tell you that record prices at the pump, skyrocketing health care costs and the rising cost of college in the face of falling or flat wages, are squeezing hard-working Texans in my Houston-based Congressional District as they struggle to make ends meet.

That is why I support increasing the minimum wage. For Texas workers the basic cost of living is rising; it is only fair that the pay for hard-working Texans does too. Nearly 890,000 hard-working Texans would directly benefit from raising the federal minimum wage to $7.25 an hour, and 1,774,000 more Texans would likely benefit from the raise.

U.S. congressional representative Sheila Jackson Lee, the viewpoint's author, worked hard for passage of the Fair Minimum Wage Act of 2007.

Raising the minimum wage is vital for Texas families. At $5.15 an hour, a full-time minimum wage worker in Texas brings home $10,712 a year—nearly $6,000 below the poverty level for a family of three. An increase of $2.10 an hour would give these families a much needed additional $4,400 a year to meet critical needs such as rent, health care, food and child care. The increase in the minimum wage before us today will not allow workers to live as large as the typical CEO [chief executive officer], who now earns 821 times more than a minimum wage worker, but at least it will allow these low-wage workers to make a little better life for themselves and their families.

Helping Millions of Workers

A minimum wage increase would raise the wages of millions of workers across America:

- An estimated 6.6 million workers (5.8 percent of the workforce) would receive an increase in their hourly wage rate if the minimum wage were raised from $5.15 to $7.25 by June 2007.
- Due to "spillover effects," the 8.2 million workers (6.5 percent of the workforce) earning up to a dollar above the minimum would also be likely to benefit from an increase.

Clay Bennett, *The Christian Science Monitor.*

Raising the minimum wage will benefit working families:

- The earnings of minimum wage workers are crucial to their families' well-being. Evidence from the 1996–97 minimum wage increase shows that the average minimum wage worker brings home more than half (54 percent) of his or her family's weekly earnings.
- An estimated 760,000 single mothers with children under 18 would benefit from a minimum wage increase to $7.25 by June 2007.
- Single mothers would benefit disproportionately from an increase—single mothers are 10.4 percent of workers affected by an increase, but they make up only 5.3 percent of the overall workforce. Approximately 1.8 million parents with children under 18 would benefit.

Contrary to popular myths and urban legends, adults make up the largest share of workers who would benefit from a minimum wage increase:

- Eighty percent of workers whose wages would be raised by a minimum wage increase to $7.25 by June 2007 are adults (age 20 or older).
- More than half (54 percent) of workers who would benefit from a minimum wage increase work full time and another third (34.5 percent) work between 20 and 34 hours per week.
- Minimum wage increases benefit disadvantaged workers and women are the largest group of beneficiaries from a minimum wage increase: 60.6 percent of workers who would benefit from an increase to $7.25 by 2007 are women.
- An estimated 7.3 percent of working women would benefit directly from that increase in the minimum wage.

The Poorest Would Benefit

A disproportionate share of minorities would benefit from a minimum wage increase:

- African Americans represent 11.1 percent of the total workforce, but are 15.3 percent of workers affected by an increase.
- Similarly, 13.4 percent of the total workforce is Hispanic, but Hispanics are 19.7 percent of workers affected by an increase.

The benefits of the increase disproportionately help those working households at the bottom of the income scale:

- Although households in the bottom 20 percent received only 5.1 percent of national income, 38.1 percent of the benefits of a minimum wage increase to $7.25 would go to these workers.
- The majority of the benefits (58.5 percent) of an increase would go to families with working, prime-aged adults in the bottom 40 percent of the income distribution.
- Among families with children and a low-wage worker affected by a minimum wage increase to $7.25, the affected worker contributes, on average, half of the family's earnings. Thirty-six percent of such workers actually contribute 100 percent of their family's earnings.

A minimum wage increase would help reverse the trend of declining real wages for low-wage workers. Between 1979 and 1989, the minimum wage lost 31 percent of its real value. By contrast, between 1989 and 1997, the minimum wage was raised four times and recovered about one-third of the value it lost in the 1980s.

Income inequality has been increasing, in part, because of the declining real value of the minimum wage. Today, the minimum wage is 33 percent of the average hourly wage of American workers, the lowest level since 1949. A minimum wage increase is part of a broad strategy to end poverty. As welfare reform forces more poor families to rely on their earnings from low-paying jobs, a minimum wage increase is likely to have a greater impact on reducing poverty.

EVALUATING THE AUTHOR'S ARGUMENTS:

Most of the viewpoint you have just read is a compilation of statistics about the minimum wage and who would benefit from it, but Sheila Jackson Lee begins her argument by referring to a biblical story and then to a story about a waitress. Why do you think she begins this way? How do these stories affect the way you read the viewpoint?

Raising the Minimum Wage Would Not Help the Poor

April L. Watkins

"Sadly, a few dollars more per hour will not bring these folks out of poverty."

In the following viewpoint April L. Watkins argues that raising the federal minimum wage will not help the working poor. Most minimum-wage earners, she contends, are not adults supporting families but young people who are unlikely to spend more income wisely. A raise in minimum wage would increase the burdens on businesses, she concludes, when it would be more appropriate to encourage low-wage workers to take responsibility for educating themselves so they can qualify for better jobs. Watkins is a public relations consultant, journalist and editor. She maintains a blog, Why It Matters, where this viewpoint originally appeared.

AS YOU READ, CONSIDER THE FOLLOWING QUESTIONS:

1. What happens to the high school dropout rates when the minimum wage is increased, according to research cited in the viewpoint?
2. What is meant by the term "unskilled labor," as it is used in the viewpoint?
3. According to the viewpoint, what is the true incentive for raising the minimum wage?

April L. Watkins, "The Misconception of Minimum Wage," Why It Matters: Decoding The Political Chatter, February 3, 2007. Reproduced by permission of the author.

As the politicians debate the pros and cons of raising the mandated federal minimum wage, I find myself a bit dazed. My first thought is "What do these folks know about minimum wage?" I dare say, very few of the good people on Capitol Hill deal with minimum wage issues in their lives or those of their family. Even fewer deal with businesses as owners who are struggling with this issue from a different angle. Either way it comes back to my question, "What do they know?" I have read reams of reports issued by both sides of the aisle, the pros and cons. Most of the findings are mindless statistics that can be manipulated to read either way you like. Some of the findings, however, touched on a concept that may be the Rosetta stone of this issue. And believe it or not, it is *not* helping the working poor. Let's look at the arguments.

On the *Pro side*, we have the obvious—more money in the pockets of American workers. We all like that idea. Studies from The Economic Policy Institute report that women would be the largest group of beneficiaries from an increase in minimum wages, with African-Americans and Hispanics taking a larger, disproportionate share as [there are] more minimum wage workers from those ethnicities. It further clarifies that an increase helps the working households at the lowest rung of the economic scale; however these households are only producing 5% of the national income. An increase in the wage would help provide a real "living wage" for these workers to combat inflation costs.

On the *Con side*, researchers at Michigan State University along with the Federal Reserve confirm that raising the minimum wage has historically adversely affected the school drop-out rates. Studies from The Heritage Foundation cite statistics that show the majority of the minimum wage workers (53%) are between the ages of 16 and 24. As kids earn more money, they are

FAST FACT

The official U.S. poverty level in 2008 was $21,200 a year for a family of four and $17,600 for a family of three. A worker earning the 2008 minimum wage of $6.55 an hour over a forty-hour week would earn less than $14,000 in a year.

Who Earns Minimum Wage?

The chart identifies employed wage and salary workers, aged sixteen and above, who were paid hourly rates with earnings at or below the prevailing federal minimum wage in 2007.

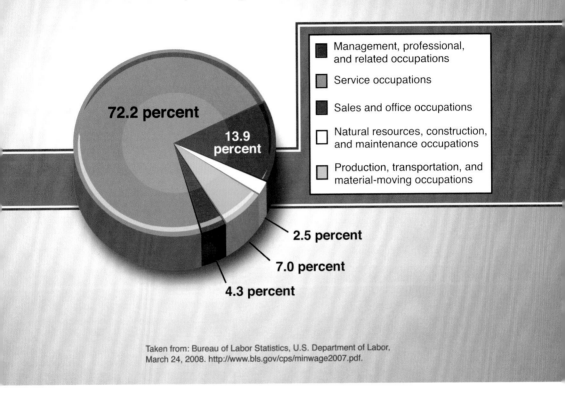

72.2 percent

13.9 percent

2.5 percent

7.0 percent

4.3 percent

- ■ Management, professional, and related occupations
- ▨ Service occupations
- ■ Sales and office occupations
- ☐ Natural resources, construction, and maintenance occupations
- ▨ Production, transportation, and material-moving occupations

Taken from: Bureau of Labor Statistics, U.S. Department of Labor, March 24, 2008. http://www.bls.gov/cps/minwage2007.pdf.

less likely to look at their long-term prospects and instead opt for short-term gratifications, such as cars, clothes and spending money.

The Minimum Wage Hurts Business

From the business perspective there is yet another view stating that companies have limits to their budgets and if forced with higher wages for unskilled labor, they will be forced to cut hours or cut labor. In looking at the various arguments for and against, several realizations popped off the page at me.

Let's start with the business view. Lately, a lot of media coverage has been given to the perceived "slave labor" state for many workers at such places as WalMart, which pays at or just above the minimum wage, with little or no benefits. One point to remember is that most of these jobs are considered "unskilled labor" positions, meaning the job requires little to no training for a worker to adequately perform the task.

Secondly, we live in a *free market economy*—people are not *forced* to work at any particular place for any particular wage. While the employment compensation and benefit policies of large corporations such as WalMart may leave much to be desired, they are at least providing jobs in America. As we have all seen, many companies have chosen to outsource their jobs to other countries.

Now let's focus on the social aspect. This is where my eyes were opened. Many of the studies both for and against the hike in minimum wage mentioned its relation to welfare. There are reports stating how raising the minimum wage will assist in shrinking the welfare rolls. By raising the minimum wage to a "living wage," it allows welfare recipients to find a job that will provide them with about the same benefits as their welfare income. AHA! The *truth* of this matter is beginning to dawn. The real case for the hike in minimum wage has nothing much to do with helping the working poor. All of the studies show that the poorer, uneducated classes will continue to live in a state of poverty without a change in their education and, thus skilled labor options. Sadly, a few dollars more per hour will not bring these folks out of poverty. The true incentive for raising the minimum wage is an attempt to help decrease the welfare rolls by providing a means of income that is at least equal to the benefits currently received by their welfare status. Thus, leaving more tax dollars for other spending and effectively shifting this burden onto businesses.

Blunt but Simple

In 1999, I came upon this same quandary after attending a Chamber of Commerce day seminar on the health benefits in my home county. After some research and number crunching, I was stunned to discover that folks who were receiving all welfare benefits (food stamps, TennCare [Tennessee's Medicaid program], etc.) received the equivalent of around $7.20/hour; while folks working for minimum wage only received $5.15/hour and usually with no medical benefits. I thought to myself, "Why would anyone want to find a minimum wage job when you were paid more to stay on welfare?" That just didn't and still doesn't make sense to me. Setting a standard for a minimum living wage is a noble cause; likewise, helping the poor is a noble cause. But . . . we help no one when we don't speak in real terms.

The message that our politicians need to send to our American workforce may be blunt, but is very simple: "As a people we are vastly under-educated compared to most developed countries. Our skills

Studies show that poverty will persist—even if the minimum wage is raised—unless poor workers are able to further their education to acquire the skills necessary for higher-paying jobs.

are outdated in this new computer technological world in which we now reside. We live in a global marketplace and salaries are based on worth to the business and value to the customer. If we want better pay . . . then we must better ourselves, educate ourselves, and learn new marketable skills."

Instead, our politicians spout those same old lines of "I'll fix it for you" to get votes. Unfortunately, the *promise* of better pay is short-lived for an unskilled labor force. Let's not rely on the politicians to make our lives better. Instead, let's follow the example of our forefathers who carved their way across this uncharted land with no help from crown or government and secure our futures by bettering ourselves and setting examples for our children. And that is . . . Why It Matters.

EVALUATING THE AUTHORS' ARGUMENTS:

April L. Watkins begins the viewpoint you have just read by observing that many statistics "can be manipulated to read either way you like." In the previous viewpoint, Sheila Jackson Lee lists many statistics to support her argument. How does the presence or lack of statistics affect whether or not you are persuaded by an argument? Do you think that the audience each author is addressing influenced her decision to use or not use statistics?

Mentoring Should Replace Welfare

Ted Abram

"Rather than a social worker that originally was educated to develop and mold a better citizen, a mentor is a friend that assists a friend."

In the following viewpoint Ted Abram demonstrates that nongovernmental mentoring programs can help people escape poverty by helping them find and keep employment. These mentoring programs are successful, he argues, because they respect the talents and the goals of their clients, unlike government programs, which promote passivity and compliance. He concludes that welfare recipients can become more productive by learning to take responsibility for their own choices with the guidance of strong mentors. Abram, a former circuit court judge for the state of Oregon, is the executive director of the American Institute for Full Employment.

AS YOU READ, CONSIDER THE FOLLOWING QUESTIONS:

1. What four simple skills are important for gaining and keeping a job, according to the viewpoint?
2. What is the name of the public housing project where Kimi Gray lived, as reported in the viewpoint?
3. According to the viewpoint, what became of Kimi Gray's five children?

Ted Abram, "The Sad History of Welfare in Modern America," Conservative Institute of M.R. Štefánik, March 9, 2006. Reproduced by permission.

The 1996 Welfare Reform, setting time limits and requiring work, changed behavior. Welfare recipients, predominately women, obtained employment and increased their income. As income has increased, poverty for the mother and her children declined. The explosive growth of out of wedlock and teen birth-rates stopped. . . .

Besides the government emphasis on work, secular and religious organizations are beginning to develop separate programs. Focusing on assisting the whole person, groups are forming to mentor the poor. Often working with the most difficult, the homeless and friendless. The most effective programs are programs that develop simple work skills, e.g., honesty, dependability, civility, and cooperation. More important these community organizations provide a mentor that assists the client in the transition to employment. Mentoring takes many forms. Kimi Gray, a former welfare recipient, mentored her associates in public housing all by herself. Cincinnati Works, a secular work placement organization, has job coaches that train, place and follow-up with employers and clients. Jobs for Life uses biblical text to train people for employment, and then has a member of the church "walk" with the client for 18 months as they transition into work and self-directed lives. These groups are having excellent results in securing and maintaining employment.

A mentor is a neighbor that guides and counsels a person. A mentor is a friend that assists a person in making decisions concerning work, education, family and community. Rather than a social worker that originally was educated to develop and mold a better citizen, a mentor is a friend that assists a friend to develop their skills and cope with the vagaries of life.

What caused the revival of mentors and self-help organizations? The community (regular people—not politicians, academics or policy experts) recognized their neighbors had been lured into a life of indifference and disrespect for themselves. Thus, neighbors observing the dysfunction of their neighbors began mentoring friends and developing organizations.

Why did the government program fail? America spent twice as much on the War on Poverty than it did to fight World War II, but it failed and harmed generations of adults and children. It failed because the premise was wrong. A neutral government social worker cannot mold and develop a better citizen. . . .

Kimi Gray

Kimi was a very large African-American woman. Kimi had five children by the time she was 19 years of age and had no stable man in her or her children's life. By the time she was in her mid-thirties, Kimi was living in a deteriorated public-housing project (Kenilworth

Many local community organizations provide mentors to assist the unemployed in developing work skills, finding jobs, and making career decisions.

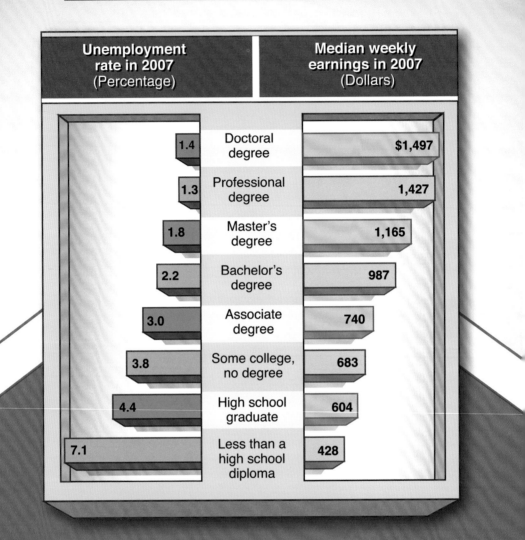

The Effects of Education on Employment

Unemployment rate in 2007 (Percentage)		Median weekly earnings in 2007 (Dollars)
1.4	Doctoral degree	$1,497
1.3	Professional degree	1,427
1.8	Master's degree	1,165
2.2	Bachelor's degree	987
3.0	Associate degree	740
3.8	Some college, no degree	683
4.4	High school graduate	604
7.1	Less than a high school diploma	428

Taken from: "Employment Predictions," Bureau of Labor Statistics, 2008. (Bureau of Labor Statistics, Current Population Survey.) www.bls.gov/emp/emptab7.htm.

Parkside), teeming with uneducated and unemployed mothers with many children. Men occasionally visited their girl friends, usually bringing drugs and violence.

Recognizing that work was essential to being a free and self-directed person, Kimi educated, organized and led her fellow residents from poverty to productivity; from recipients of public housing to ownership; from fear of her neighbors to living in a stable and nurturing community; from children without fathers to children with participating fathers. Kimi Gray assisted individuals, families and her community to becoming productive and choosing their life careers. Why was Kimi successful? She recognized and appreciated that every person has talents, and can organize and control their lives, be productive and be a significant member of society.

How did Kimi lead this transformation? First, Kimi locked the public housing managers out and took over running the project. Next Kimi went to neighbors and asked, "what are your desires, what do you want to do, how do you want to live?" Kimi appreciated the value and rewards of work.

A few years ago, Kimi related to me how she started with her neighbors. The following is paraphrased: "I asked her what she wanted to be. She wanted to be a nurse. I next asked if she could read or write. She couldn't. Then I made a deal with her. I would teach her to read and write and she would work as an orderly in the local hospital. Next I went to the hospital and talked with the management. I was blunt. I told them they had two choices. Either hire my neighbor or they would see her repeatedly in the operating room as a non-paying patient. The hospital hired her."

Gradually Kimi's neighbors became employed and learned to read and write, to organize and direct their lives. Kimi and her neighbors at Kenilworth

> ## FAST FACT
>
> According to the organization Mentor, 3 million young people in the United States are involved in high-quality formal mentoring relationships. The organization estimates that 14.6 million more young people need mentors.

Parkside convinced the federal government to sell them the public housing. Instead of receiving free housing they became owners. It was through ownership of, responsibility for, and control of their housing that Kimi believed residents would improve their education, economic well-being and family functioning. Kimi was correct and at the time of her death in 2000, Kenilworth Parkside had an average of more than one college student per unit in the 464-unit development.

Welfare Creates Dependency

In 1993, as welfare reform was just beginning in the United States of America, Kimi wrote the following about America's welfare system and its effects:

> Welfare helps people get by but in doing so it programs them to be dependent. First it predicts, then enables, then dictates dependent behavior. It assumes you will be satisfied with a handout, as though living on the dole is all you're good for.
>
> Well, I'm good for a lot more than that, and so is everyone I know. When I was 19, I was a single mother with five children living on welfare in a run-down, crime-ridden public housing project in Washington, D.C.
>
> Now, 28 years later, I still live in the same location, but it's a different place. That public housing project is now a residential development owned and operated by its residents. Crime is virtually non-existent, teenage pregnancies are rare, and few of the residents are on welfare, and then only for a short time.
>
> I am president of the Kenilworth Parkside Resident Management Corporation, a multi-million dollar property management firm, and my five children all are college graduates and productive citizens.
>
> As we residents of Kenilworth Parkside fought our way out of poverty we found that the biggest barrier to our progress was the welfare system itself; a morass of rules and regulations that penalized us if we got jobs, formed families, or tried to create small businesses or meet our own social, health, and educational service needs.
>
> The anti-work, anti-family welfare rules are still in place, and the bureaucrats are still there to make life miserable for anyone who dares to dream of escaping the poverty trap.

Kimi was a very talented and gifted person, and it is unreasonable to expect all persons on public assistance to be so successful. However, the thousands of welfare recipients she assisted had a variety of talents and backgrounds. Kimi's approach was successful because her knowledge of people and poverty is universal. People do have talents; people will make positive choices and will become productive citizens.

EVALUATING THE AUTHOR'S ARGUMENTS:

After Ted Abram describes the success of Kimi Gray's program in the viewpoint you have just read, he acknowledges that it is "unreasonable" to expect all programs to do so well. What is the value of an example that is not typical? When proposing an alternative, is it useful to show the best possible outcome? Explain your answer.

The Family Security Framework Should Replace Welfare

Shelley Waters Boots, Jennifer Macomber, and Anna Danziger

"Unless policymakers also help enable parents to care for their children and address their needs, work may seem like or be a losing proposition."

In the following viewpoint researchers Shelley Waters Boots, Jennifer Macomber, and Anna Danziger propose a "Family Security policy framework," a new approach to welfare policies. The government should support affordable day care and parental time away from work, they argue, to help low-income parents care for their children without jeopardizing their jobs. They conclude that unless policy makers focus more on the well-being of children, requiring parents to find work will hurt as much as it helps. Boots is a senior fellow at the Urban Institute; Macomber and Danziger work with the institute's Center on Labor, Human Services, and Population.

AS YOU READ, CONSIDER THE FOLLOWING QUESTIONS:
  1. What are children's four key needs, as outlined in the viewpoint?

Shelley Waters Boots, Jennifer Macomber, and Anna Danziger, "Family Security: Supporting Parents' Employment and Children's Development," *Urban Institute New Safety Net Paper 3*, July 1, 2008. Reproduced by permission.

2. According to tax policy expert Gene Steuerle, what percentage of the country's gross domestic product is spent on children?
3. Who would pay for paid sick leave and paid family leave under the Family Security approach, according to the viewpoint?

Since the passage of welfare reform more than a decade ago, the new safety net's mainstay has been enabling parents to work. Today, 7 in 10 low-income families have at least one working parent. Yet, unless policymakers also help enable parents to care for their children and address their needs, work may seem like or be a losing proposition. While the competing priorities of family and work are front and center in the lives of parents, in the policy world issues of parental work and children's developmental needs are frequently in separate spheres. Too often, public discourse on how to encourage work among low-income families never touches on what growing children need to develop and succeed.

Below, we focus on the needs of children in low-income working families and put forth a new policy framework that integrates and supports work and children's development. Drawing on a vast literature on children's well-being and development, we assert that children have four key needs—stability, health, nurturing, and activity—that must inform any policy approach intended to support and encourage parental work. We also remind policymakers of research showing that disadvantaged children can benefit substantially from programs that address their development needs.

Little Time for Child Care

Low-income working parents struggle with the same challenges other working parents do but have far fewer resources, more vulnerabilities, and less flexible jobs. For example, for low-income working families, shift work and changing schedules make it harder to stabilize meal and bedtime routines. Lack of paid leave challenges parents to make and keep their children's regular doctor or dental visits. Parental work in the first months of a child's life may make it hard for a newborn to form critical attachments to a parent. Similarly, lack of workplace flexibility can keep parents from attending school events regularly and

Not All Workers Find Scheduling Flexibility

Most low-wage earners do not have the flexibility in their work schedules to take children to school or day care or to doctor's appointments.

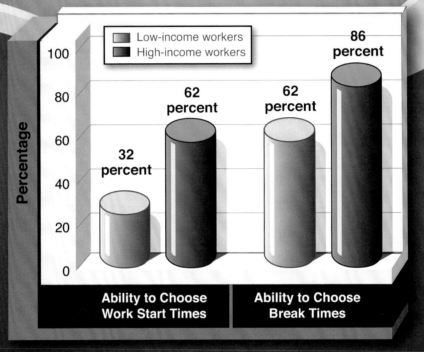

Taken from: Shelley Waters Boots, Jennifer Macomber, and Anna Danziger, "Family Security: Supporting Parents' Employment and Children's Development," The Urban Institute, *New Safety Net Paper 3*, July 2008.

having more than perfunctory conversations with their children. And cash-strapped parents are hard pressed to pay for quality child care or camps, lessons, and social activities.

One in four children in low-income families have parents who work full time. Specifically, in 2007, 7.7 million low-income children lived in families where either a single parent worked full time or both parents in two-parent married families did. Some 1.1 million of these children were under age 3. Their parents work long and hard but still have little income or time to devote to their children. Many in lower-paying jobs do not have the flexibility parents need to care for their children when they are first born or sick, much less meet the extraordinary demands of kids with disabilities or special needs.

To help low-income parents help their children, we propose a new policy framework—Family Security—that encourages and supports parents' work but also promotes the healthy development of their children. Our plan reflects a growing concern among both children's advocates and, more recently, economists about the need to invest in children. As Nobel Laureate James Heckman puts it, "investing in disadvantaged young children is a rare public policy initiative with no equity-efficiency tradeoff. It reduces the inequality associated with the accident of birth and at the same time raises the productivity of society at large." Research by tax policy expert Gene Steuerle reveals that a mere 2.6 percent of GDP [gross domestic product] is spent on children, and that is expected to decrease further as entitlement programs grow. "As the kids' share of the budget shrinks and we invest in them proportionately less," says Steuerle," how can we expect them later to earn the money to pay the taxes to cover our ballooning pile of retirement and health benefits?" . . .

Triple Dividends for Families

As put forth below, our Family Security policy framework rests on a summary of children's four key needs. Through this lens, we propose three policy options that allow parents to work and meet their children's needs: making quality child care affordable, offering parental leave time to care for children, and providing low-income people with comprehensive family services. Some policies have double or triple, if indirect, dividends. For example, paid leave that allows parents to leave work to care for a sick child directly addresses the child's health needs, but it also allows the parent to stay employed when illness strikes the family; in turn, that enables parents to keep paying rent or making mortgage payments and thus to spare the child potentially jarring moves. Such multi-impact policies create an environment in which parents can work and raise children who will thrive. . . .

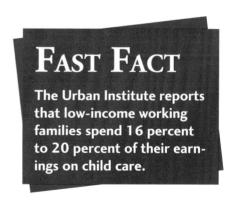

FAST FACT

The Urban Institute reports that low-income working families spend 16 percent to 20 percent of their earnings on child care.

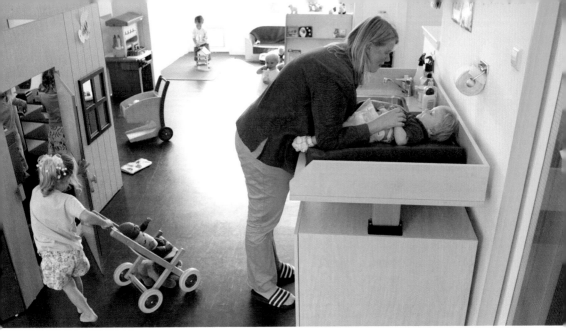

Some children's advocates argue that the government should support a safety net of services for children of low-income workers, including affordable day care.

The Family Security approach would provide good, affordable child care so parents can work without undermining their children's development. Our approach would accomplish the three goals that any new policy proposals in this area must meet. First is affordability for a much larger portion of families in the United States. Although all parents would pay something for care, low-income working families would have limited co-payments. Second is redress of the market failures that limit the quality of care that families can get through subsidies or the broader market. Third is federal provision of more and better coordinated after-school care. . . .

The Family Security approach would help parents balance the demands of work and caregiving when they need to be away from work to address their children's needs. We suggest three key supports to address parents' need for time to care: flexible work, employer-financed paid sick leave, and employee-financed paid family leave. . . .

Shared Responsibility for Children

A single advantage of our approach is that every sector of society is expected to contribute to advancing families and investing in our nation's next generation. Parents are required to work, using their skills and productivity to keep our economy growing. Government repairs parts of the work support system that are currently failing families and children by investing more in a high-quality child-care system that parents and employers can rely on, additional after-school programs, and Head Start and Early Head Start. And employers start a dialogue with their employees on new ways to work and make modest investments in paid sick leave so employees can care for themselves or their family members when illness strikes. We also assume that our proposed new labor standard will be more palatable to employers if, as Urban Institute colleagues propose, a new health care system obviates a significant portion of the rising health expenses that employers now shoulder.

Besides spreading responsibility among all who stand to benefit—except for the children themselves—our proposals help leverage current programs and resources, many with different goals and targeted constituencies. We connect traditionally disconnected policies, integrating those focused on parents' work with those focused on children's development. We emphasize "family" security rather than parent or child security in the hope that it blends a focus on parents' needs with those of children, rather than thinking of them distinctly. Finally, we try to bridge child care as a work support and child care in support of child development. Despite research that shows a need for such bridge-building, policy conversations about both work and family have remained fragmented. We believe that low-income working families will fare better if policy analysts think more creatively and comprehensively about how to meet both parents' and children's needs.

EVALUATING THE AUTHORS' ARGUMENTS:

The two previous viewpoints have mentioned the financial cost of fighting poverty, although neither emphasizes money. Ted Abram compares the cost of the War on Poverty with that of World War II, implying that the United States has spent too much on poverty; Shelley Waters Boots and her colleagues cite the percentage of GDP that is spent to help children, implying that the United States has spent too little. Which viewpoint is more persuasive on the issue of spending? Why?

The British System Has Reduced Child Poverty

"[Britain's] policy-driven focus on reducing child poverty has helped to ensure that economic growth is reaching those at the bottom of the income scale."

Jared Bernstein and Mark Greenberg

In the following viewpoint Jared Bernstein and Mark Greenberg examine a British plan to eliminate child poverty by 2020. Because the number of poor children in Great Britain has decreased since the year 2000 while the number in the United States has increased, they argue that the United States should adopt at least some of the British programs. Seriously targeting poverty would be a good way for the U.S. government to regain its reputation as a positive force, they conclude. Bernstein is a senior economist at the Economic Policy Institute, and Greenberg is executive director of the Task Force on Poverty for the Center for American Progress.

AS YOU READ, CONSIDER THE FOLLOWING QUESTIONS:

1. As reported in the viewpoint, by how much did Great Britain hope to reduce child poverty by 2005? Was that target reached?
2. How has the British government increased the incomes of working parents, according to the viewpoint?
3. Why do British politicians cited in the viewpoint think that the target date is important, even if it is not reached?

For anyone interested in reducing child poverty, there was heartening bad news out of Britain [in March 2006]. In 1999 the Blair government introduced an initiative to end child poverty by 2020, with an initial goal of cutting it by one-quarter by April of [2005]. Recently the government reported that it missed that target: The number of children in poverty dropped by "only" about 17 percent—some 700,000 kids over the past five years.

If only we could have such problems in this country.

Since 2000 the number of American children living in poverty has risen 12 percent—to 13 million. The initial growth was due to the economic downturn. But since then, despite the ongoing expansion, the poverty rate for children on this side of the pond keeps rising, largely because the benefits of the recovery have flowed so disproportionately to families at the top of the income scale.

But in the United Kingdom [UK], the policy-driven focus on reducing child poverty has helped to ensure that economic growth is reaching those at the bottom of the income scale. Yes, they've missed an interim target, and some parts of the plan need rethinking, but they're making progress while we're backsliding.

A National Directive

This all started back in 1999, when Prime Minister Tony Blair gave a speech in which he set the goal of eliminating child poverty by 2020. As we learned on a recent trip there to see how things were unfolding, the officials at the relevant agencies don't claim to know all the answers. But with a directive to end poverty in 20 years, they rolled up their sleeves and got to work.

Members of Parliament and the Blair government built, and continue to build, a comprehensive system designed to boost the incomes of working parents, mainly through subsidies to low-wage earners. They raised the minimum wage and have continued to push it up regularly.

> ## FAST FACT
>
> According to a survey conducted by Great Britain's Department for Work and Pensions, 41 percent of the British public believes there is "very little" child poverty in the country. In fact, while progress has been made, more than 3 million British children are still poor.

In 1999 British prime minister Tony Blair and his government designed a comprehensive system designed to end child poverty in Britain by the year 2020.

They're in the midst of implementing a 10-year national child-care strategy designed to help parents get access to affordable, high-quality child care (to make it easier for them to hold down a job), and they instituted programs to develop healthy and school-ready preschoolers, teens and young adults.

They launched a cabinet-level government agency, the Social Exclusion Unit, to deal with the combination of problems that interact to keep families poor: a lack of marketable skills, chronic unemployment, poor housing in high-crime areas and so on.

As revealed in the recent reports, there have been problems. One critic pointed out that with 11 agency departments responsible for the initiative, efforts have been too diffuse. Getting the right tax credits to the right workers hasn't always gone smoothly, and some parts of the program, such as access to reliable child care, need expanding.

But what's amazing about all this is that elected officials in a major advanced economy decided to try to do something about a trend they viewed as unjust and ultimately harmful to the prospects of their society.

Child Poverty in Rich Nations

The graph shows the percentage of children under the age of eighteen who live in households with a total income of less than 50 percent of the national median.

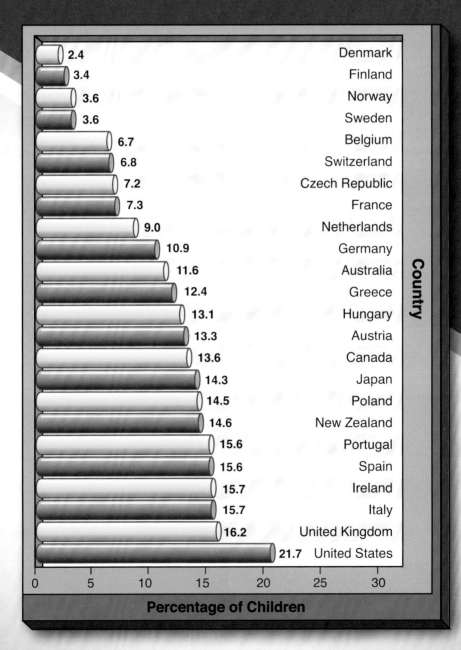

Country	Percentage of Children
Denmark	2.4
Finland	3.4
Norway	3.6
Sweden	3.6
Belgium	6.7
Switzerland	6.8
Czech Republic	7.2
France	7.3
Netherlands	9.0
Germany	10.9
Australia	11.6
Greece	12.4
Hungary	13.1
Austria	13.3
Canada	13.6
Japan	14.3
Poland	14.5
New Zealand	14.6
Portugal	15.6
Spain	15.6
Ireland	15.7
Italy	15.7
United Kingdom	16.2
United States	21.7

Taken from: *Child Poverty in Perspective: An Overview of Child Well-Being in Rich Countries,* Innocenti Report Card 7, 2007. UNICEF Innocenti Research Centre, Florence, Italy.

Focusing on the Target

As we learned in our meetings with those whose job it is to hit these goals, opponents initially warned that investing significant national resources in ending child poverty was incompatible with global competition. We asked one politician about this. His response: "How can the U.K. compete globally if a third of our children grow up poor?"

What if you don't end child poverty by the targeted date of 2020, we asked. The question didn't really interest them. The target, they argued, focused the minds of the politicians, the agencies and the public. Without it, they would never have gotten as far as they have. In fact, upon release of the news about missing the target, John Hutton, a Blair cabinet Secretary, promised to "redouble" the government's efforts to hit the target.

The more you learn about this initiative, the more you realize just how far off track we've gotten. It's hard to imagine that anyone in high office in this country would get near an idea like this right now. Yet it's exactly the kind of idea that might revitalize government as a positive force for making a lasting difference in the lives of our most vulnerable citizens.

Is it even conceivable that we could adapt such a target here? Absolutely. In fact, a spate of recent news stories has pointed out that a major national party whose name begins with D is in desperate need of a big, unifying idea. What's bloody wrong with this one?

EVALUATING THE AUTHORS' ARGUMENTS:

In the viewpoint you have just read, the authors make two comparisons: They compare the success of the British child-poverty plan with the original goals of the plan, and they compare the success of the British plan with the success of programs in the United States. What do you believe is the purpose of this strategy? How does knowing that the British plan falls somewhat short of its own targets affect your belief that such a plan should be tried in the United States?

The French System Supports Low-Tier Workers

"French parents at all income levels get a great deal of government assistance with childcare and health care."

Karen Seccombe

In the following viewpoint sociologist Karen Seccombe argues that the United States could improve its care of all citizens by modeling its programs on those of France. In many ways the United States and France are similar, she explains, but fewer French families struggle to pay for housing, health care, and child care because their government helps cover those costs for citizens at all income levels. The United States could provide more care for its citizens, she concludes, if it simply shifted its priorities. Seccombe is a sociology professor in the Portland State University School of Community Health.

AS YOU READ, CONSIDER THE FOLLOWING QUESTIONS:

1. How do the unemployment rates of France and the United States compare, according to the viewpoint?
2. Why, according to the viewpoint, is there no shame attached to receiving government assistance in France?
3. In order to equal France's spending on child well-being, how much more would the United States have to spend, according to economist Barbara Bergmann?

France is one country out of many that can provide a rich contrast to the United States. In the book *Saving Our Children From Poverty*, economist Barbara Bergmann notes that there are many demographic and economic similarities between the two nations. The annual rate of growth is comparable, and both countries have similar rates of female labor force participation and births outside of marriage, and have minority populations of comparable proportions. France has a 50 percent higher unemployment rate, yet their poverty rate is considerably less than that of the United States. The child poverty rate is 6 percent in France compared to 22 percent in the United States. Moreover, about a quarter of single mothers in France receive welfare-type benefits, compared to two-thirds of single mothers in the United States. The reason for these differences is that France has made a successful commitment to enhance low-tier work. They have improved the conditions surrounding these jobs so that they are no longer necessarily associated with low wages, and they do not automatically reduce the array of benefits that are vital to an individual's and a family's well-being.

Fast Fact

In France, the minimum wage is reset annually by the government. By law, the minimum wage must increase by at least the rate of inflation for the previous year.

Available by Right

This investment in low-tier work is not only monetary, but is reflected in their entire orientation to caring for their citizens. French parents at all income levels get a great deal of government assistance with childcare and health care, for example. Childcare is provided by an educated work force, and it is considered valued and important work. Free public nursery schools are available for children ages two-and-a-half through six, and by the time they are three years old, virtually 100 percent of French children attend. There is also a well coordinated before- and after-school care program for a nominal fee. Likewise, free health care is available to everyone by right of citizenship, and it is not lost when a person loses a job, develops an illness that is expensive to treat, or leaves welfare. The French government supplements the income of families with children by providing family allowances, housing assistance, and cash payments to pregnant women. These programs are not limited to poor families, unemployed families, or single parents. Moreover, because most of these programs are universal and available regardless of income, they have little or no stigma attached to them. They are considered to be normal facets of their social structure, much in the way public education is in our country. These programs are rights of all citizens, not privileges, and therefore there is no shame in receiving them. In contrast, in the United States we have families who need assistance, but either do not know what is available, do not know how to access it, or have been so absorbed

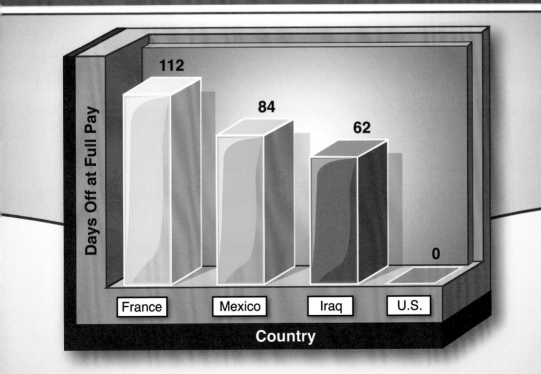

Paid Maternity Leave

Most nations offer women time off at full pay to care for newborn babies. The United States is one of only a few countries that do not offer any form of paid parental leave.

Taken from: United Nations Statistics Division, 2005. http://unstats.un.org/
unsd/demographic/products/indwm/ww2005/tab5c.htm.

In France, all low-income workers receive substantial government assistance, which means that families like this one do not find themselves struggling to pay for housing, health care, and child care.

by the Individualist perspective that their ego or guilt prevents them from seeking help that they qualify for and need.

Workers in France with low wages get even more help from these and other programs. For example, a single mother in France who moves from welfare to work retains $6,000 in government cash and housing grants. She would continue to receive free health insurance and would pay a negligible amount for childcare, as do all French citizens. She would not have to face the hardships associated with low-tier work as do her sisters in the United States. Thus, despite the fact that the welfare programs in France are more generous than are ours, women are still more likely to leave them to pursue jobs. They can do this because of the security that the French government provides to all its workers. It is wrong to assume that we must have a punitive approach and keep benefits low so that women will not abuse the welfare system. Here, as in France, women would prefer employment, and they will work, if they continue to have the security that they need to care for their families.

Spending Priorities

Critics may scoff that the costs for these programs are prohibitive. According to data compiled by Bergmann, the United States would need to spend approximately 59 percent more than its current level to increase our spending on programs for child well-being to that of the French. As the richest country in the world, with one of the lowest tax rates, investing in our families in this fashion is not an impossibility. Instead, our money is being spent in other ways—it is a matter of priority. For example, the United States spends over twice as much money on defense as it does for programs that promote children's well-being (e.g., childcare and development, income supplements, income tax reductions, medical care for low-income children), whereas in France, the opposite occurs. We also spend an inordinate amount of money on the enforcement of our new punitive policies. That money would be better spent reinforcing the security of the vulnerable members of our society, which, despite our comfort in thinking to the contrary, could be any one of us.

EVALUATING THE AUTHOR'S ARGUMENTS:

In the viewpoint you have just read, Karen Seccombe describes some of the demographic and economic similarities between France and the United States. She does not, however, describe philosophical differences between the French and the American people. What basic beliefs do many Americans share that would make changing to the French system difficult?

Editor's note: These facts can be used in reports or papers to reinforce or add credibility when making important points or claims.

Americans Looking for Help

The Kaiser Family Foundation Health Tracking Poll: Election 2008, conducted in October 2008, revealed:

- Thirty-nine percent of respondents found that recent changes in the economy had made paying for gas a "serious problem."
- Thirty-five percent reported serious problems getting a well-paying job or a raise in pay.
- Twenty-eight percent reported serious problems paying for health care and health insurance.
- Twenty-two percent reported serious problems paying for food.
- Thirty-two percent of respondents reported that their family had had trouble paying medical bills in the year leading up to October 2008. In September 2006, only 25 percent of respondents had reported the same problems.

A survey of low-wage workers conducted during the summer of 2008 by *The Washington Post*, the Kaiser Family Foundation, and Harvard University focused on the experiences and challenges facing the lowest-paid members of the American workforce. Among its findings:

- Seventy-five percent reported that finding good jobs had gotten harder in the previous few years; 16 percent reported that their situation had not changed; and 8 percent reported that finding good jobs had become easier.
- Seventy-four percent reported that being able to afford health care had become more difficult; 15 percent reported that affordability had not changed; and 8 percent reported that it had become easier to afford health care.

- Seventy-two percent reported that it had become more difficult to get ahead financially; 17 percent reported that the situation had not changed; and 10 percent said that it had become easier to get ahead financially.
- Sixty-eight percent reported that it had become harder to find decent, affordable housing; 13 percent reported that the situation had not changed; and 14 percent reported that it had become easier to find decent, affordable housing.

The National Center for Children in Poverty (NCCP) collects data every year to determine what it costs for families to meet their basic needs. According to 2008 data:

- The 2008 federal poverty level (FPL) for a family of four is $21,200. The NCCP calculates that it actually costs an average of $42,400 for a family of four to make ends meet.
- The 2008 FPL for a family of three is $17,600. The NCCP calculates that it costs an average of $35,200 for a family of three to make ends meet.
- The 2008 FPL for a family of two is $14,000. The NCCP calculates that it costs an average of $28,000 for a family of two to make ends meet.

According to the October 2008 Hormel Hunger Survey, an annual survey of Americans' experiences with and views on hunger:

- Eighty percent of Americans reported that they were concerned about rising food prices; four out of ten were very concerned.
- Nineteen percent said that they have had to choose between buying food and buying gas.
- Fourteen percent reported that they or someone in their family have received food from a food bank, shelter, or other charitable organization in the past year because they did not have money for food; in 2007 the number was 13 percent. Six percent in 2008 said that they or someone in their family had gone to bed hungry because they could not afford food. Sixty-seven percent said that the U.S. government should make solving hunger a higher priority and should provide more funding for food assistance, the same percentage who said this in 2007.

As reported by the 2005 America's Second Harvest survey of food pantries, food kitchens, and shelter programs providing emergency food assistance:

- Of the food pantries, which distribute packaged food for use at home, 64.6 percent served more clients in 2005 than they did in 2001; 20.1 percent served about the same number of clients; and 7.1 percent served fewer clients in 2005 than they did in 2001.
- Of the food kitchens, which serve meals on-site, 61.0 percent served more clients in 2005 than they did in 2001; 25.3 percent served about the same number of clients; and 5.8 percent served fewer clients in 2005 than they did in 2001.
- Of the shelter programs, 52.4 percent served more clients with food assistance in 2005 than they did in 2001; 37.2 percent served about the same number of clients; and 4.2 percent served fewer clients in 2005 than they did in 2001.

Welfare and Other Sources of Assistance

According to a March 2007 Harris Interactive poll about the federal budget deficit:

- When asked to examine a list of twelve federal programs and pick two that should be cut if federal spending had to be reduced, the space program was chosen by 51 percent of respondents. Welfare programs were chosen by 28 percent, defense spending by 28 percent, environmental programs by 16 percent, Medicaid by 4 percent, education by 3 percent, Social Security by 2 percent and Medicare by 1 percent.

According to a July 2005 poll from the Pew Forum on Religion and Public Life:

- Sixty-six percent of Americans favor allowing churches and other houses of worship to apply, along with other organizations, for government funding to provide social services; 30 percent were opposed to this practice.
- However, 58 percent are opposed to directly shifting funds from federal antipoverty programs to religious groups in order for them to provide social services; 33 percent favor this idea.
- Even if it would mean raising taxes, 64 percent of Americans support the government guaranteeing health insurance for all Americans; 30 percent are opposed.

- Sixty-nine percent favor using government funds to provide more assistance to the poor; 25 percent are opposed.

Working and Parenting

In July 2007, the Pew Research Center surveyed adults about combining working and parenting. It found:

- Mothers who had children aged seventeen or younger at home were asked to rate the job they had done as mothers on a scale of one to ten, with ten being the highest. Of mothers who did not hold jobs outside the home, 43 percent rated themselves nine or ten; 41 percent of mothers who worked part-time rated themselves nine or ten; and 28 percent of mothers who held full-time jobs rated themselves nine or ten.
- Most of the respondents rated themselves seven or eight in terms of their performance as mothers: 49 percent of those who did not hold jobs outside the home; 54 percent of those with part-time jobs; and 65 percent of those working full-time.
- When asked to define their ideal working situation, 50 percent said that they would prefer to work part-time; 29 percent of all mothers of minor children reported that they would prefer not to work outside the home; and 20 percent would prefer to work full-time.
- Both men and women were asked whether the increase in working mothers with young children was generally a good thing or a bad thing for society. Among men, 42 percent thought it was a bad thing; 31 percent thought it did not make much difference; and 22 percent thought it was a good thing. Among women, 41 percent thought it was a bad thing; 33 percent thought it did not make much difference; and 22 percent thought it was a good thing.

Welfare and Poverty as American Priorities

In 2008, the organization Spotlight on Poverty studied news stories about poverty and readers' attitudes toward those stories leading up to the November elections. Among the findings:

- Searching for the terms "poverty," "politics," and "candidate" in news stories in major media outlets, the study found 4,344 stories in 2007 and 1,775 in 2003—a 145 percent increase in stories about how candidates for public office would address poverty.

- Searching for the terms "poverty," "politics," "candidate," and "presidential," the study found 3,217 stories in 2007 and 924 in 2003—a 248 percent increase in stories about how candidates for the presidency would address poverty.
- Nevertheless, 56 percent of respondents to a survey later in 2007 believed that the media had not "spent an adequate amount of time during the presidential campaign covering the issue of how to fight poverty in the U.S." Of those, 41.2 percent felt this way "strongly."

Glossary

Aid to Families with Dependent Children (AFDC): A federal program, generally called "welfare," that provided cash assistance to poor American families with children. AFDC was replaced in 1996 by **Temporary Assistance for Needy Families (TANF).**

Earned Income Tax Credit (EITC): A program that reduces the income tax owed by low-income working people, especially people who are supporting children. EITC is the largest antipoverty program in the United States.

entitlement program: A program that gives financial benefits to any citizen or resident who meets the eligibility requirements. In the United States, federal entitlement programs include Social Security, Medicare, and Medicaid, food stamps, unemployment insurance, and many Veterans Administration programs.

food stamps: A program offered by the U.S. Department of Agriculture's Food and Nutrition Service that provides benefits to low-income people that they can use to buy food. On October 1, 2008, the program was renamed the **Supplemental Nutrition Assistance Program (SNAP).**

Medicaid: A health insurance program that helps pay the medical bills of some but not all low-income individuals, including children, pregnant women, parents of eligible children, seniors, and people with disabilities. Because Medicaid is funded jointly by the federal government and state governments, each state has its own rules for determining who is eligible for coverage.

Medicare: A federal entitlement program that provides health insurance for all people aged sixty-five or older, and for people under age sixty-five with certain disabilities.

Personal Responsibility and Work Opportunity Reconciliation Act (PRWORA): The official name of what is usually called "welfare reform." Signed into law on August 26, 1996, PRWORA focused on the idea of "welfare-to-work" and created **Temporary Assistance for Needy Families (TANF).**

Section 8: A federal program that helps low-income people pay rent, officially called the Housing Choice Voucher Program.

State Children's Health Insurance Program (SCHIP): A federal program that gives funds to states to provide health insurance to families with children. The program covers children in families whose incomes are too low to pay for health insurance but too high to qualify for Medicaid.

Supplemental Nutrition Assistance Program: A program offered by the U.S. Department of Agriculture's Food and Nutrition Service to help low-income people buy food. Formerly known as **food stamps.**

Supplemental Security Income (SSI): A monthly cash payment to certain elderly or disabled people, based on financial need.

Temporary Assistance for Needy Families (TANF): A state-run program that provides financial assistance to families while working to help them become independent so that the assistance can end. In 1996, TANF replaced an older program, **Aid to Families with Dependent Children (AFDC)**, which provided more cash assistance with fewer rules and expectations for how recipients would use the money.

Title XIX: Another name for **Medicaid.** The Medicaid program was created in 1965 through the section called Title XIX of the Social Security Act.

WIC: The common name for the Special Supplemental Nutrition Program for Women, Infants, and Children, a federal program that helps pay for health care and food for low-income pregnant women, breastfeeding women, and infants and children under the age of five.

Organizations to Contact

The editors have compiled the following list of organizations concerned with the issues debated in this book. The descriptions are derived from materials provided by the organizations. All have publications or information available for interested readers. The list was compiled on the date of publication of the present volume; the information provided here may change. Be aware that many organizations take several weeks or longer to respond to queries, so allow as much time as possible.

Administration for Children and Families (ACF)
370 L'Enfant Prom. SW
Washington, DC 20201
(202) 401-5762
Web site: www.acf.hhs.gov

The ACF is a federal agency that funds state, territory, local, and tribal organizations to provide family assistance (welfare), child support, child care, Head Start, child welfare, and other programs relating to children and families. This official government Web site contains a series of Frequently Asked Questions about TANF and other programs, and a link for citizens in need to contact the agency and find help with other questions. The site also offers press releases and fact sheets about all of the agencies operated by the U.S. Department of Health and Human Services, as well as reports and articles about ACF's "Key Priorities," which include the Faith-Based and Community Initiative and the Healthy Marriage Initiative.

American Enterprise Institute (AEI)
1150 Seventeenth St. NW, Ste. 1100
Washington, DC 20036
(202) 862-5800
fax: (202)862-7177
Web site: www.aei.org

The American Enterprise Institute for Public Policy Research is a private, nonpartisan, not-for-profit institution dedicated to research and education on issues of government, politics, economics, and social welfare. Advocating for limited government and competitive private enterprise, it conducts research in economic policy studies, social and political studies, and defense and foreign policy studies, and supports the Welfare Reform Academy at the University of Maryland School of Public Policy. Publications available on its Web site include the articles "Social Welfare Conservatism" and "Attitudes About Welfare Reform," as well as abstracts of AEI Press books including *The Poverty of "the Poverty Rate."*

Cato Institute
1000 Massachusetts Ave. NW
Washington, DC 20001-5403
(202) 842-0200
fax (202) 842-3490
Web site: www.cato.org

Founded in 1977, the Cato Institute is a nonprofit public policy research foundation that encourages limited government, individual liberty, free markets and peace, and strives to achieve greater involvement of the public in questions of policy and the proper role of government. Research areas include Education and Child Policy; Health, Welfare, and Entitlements; Tax and Budget Policy; and others. Its online library includes reviews, journals, articles, opinion columns, videos, and policy studies, and a dedicated section for students includes blogs and an "Ask the Expert" feature.

Center for Law and Social Policy (CLASP)
1015 Fifteenth St. NW, Ste. 400
Washington, DC 20005
(202) 906-8000
fax: (202) 842-2885
Web site: www.clasp.org

CLASP is a national nonprofit organization that works to improve the economic security, educational and workforce prospects, and family stability of low-income parents, children, and youth and to secure equal justice for all. To carry out this mission, CLASP conducts research, provides policy analysis, advocates at the federal and state levels, and offers information and technical assistance on a range of family policy and equal justice issues. Through its Web site, CLASP provides transcripts of audio conferences on such topics as "Poverty and Opportunity: Developments around the Nation," and offers publications including "Protecting Children and Strengthening Families" and "Ten Years After Welfare Reform, It's Time to Make Work Work for Families."

Center on Budget and Policy Priorities
820 First St. NE, Ste. 510
Washington, DC 20002
(202) 408-1080
fax: (202) 408-1056
e-mail: center@cbpp.org
Web site: www.cbpp.org

The Center on Budget and Policy Priorities is a policy organization working at the federal and state levels on fiscal policy and public programs that affect low- and moderate-income families and individuals. The center conducts research and analysis to inform public debates over proposed budget and tax policies and to help ensure that the needs of low-income families and individuals are considered in these debates. Its Web site offers audio presentations, slide shows, and videos on topics including "Making America Stronger: U.S. Food Stamp Program," as well as annual assessments of the TANF program and "An Introduction to TANF," an illustrated report for general readers.

Coalition on Human Needs
1120 Connecticut Ave. NW, Ste. 910
Washington, DC 20036
(202) 223-2532
fax: (202) 223-2538
e-mail: info@chn.org
Web site: www.chn.org

The Coalition on Human Needs is an alliance of national organizations working together to promote adequate funding for human needs programs, progressive tax policies, and other federal measures to address the needs of low-income and other vulnerable populations. Members include civil rights, religious, labor and professional organizations, and those concerned with the well-being of children, women, the elderly, and people with disabilities. The coalition publishes an electronic newsletter, the *Human Needs Report*, and offers on its Web site a collection of articles including "Finally—Federal Minimum Wage Increase Signed into Law" and audio budget briefings.

The Heritage Foundation
214 Massachusetts Ave. NE
Washington, DC 20002
(202) 546-4400
fax: (202) 546-8328
e-mail: info@heritage.org
Web site: www.heritage.org

Founded in 1973, the Heritage Foundation is a research and educational institute whose mission is to formulate and promote conservative public policies based on the principles of free enterprise, limited government, individual freedom, traditional American values, and a strong national defense. The foundation works on a wide range of domestic and foreign issues including the economy, education, and welfare. Its Web site collects press releases, policy reports, and opinion columns, with titles including "Memo to Congress: Make Jobs, Not Work" and "Welfare Reform Turns Ten: Evidence Shows Reduced Dependence, Poverty," and offers a blog, The Foundry.

Institute for Research on Poverty (IRP)
University of Wisconsin–Madison
1180 Observatory Dr.
3412 Social Science Bldg.
Madison, WI 53706-1393
(608) 262-6358
fax: (608) 265-3119
Web site: www.irp.wisc.edu/publications/dps/dplist.htm

The IRP, sponsored by the U.S. Department of Health and Human Services, is a center for interdisciplinary research into the causes and consequences of poverty and social inequality in the United States.

Based at the University of Wisconsin–Madison, it has a particular interest in poverty and family welfare in the Midwest. The institute's affiliates, who represent a variety of disciplines, formulate and test basic theories of poverty and inequality, develop and evaluate social policy alternatives, and analyze trends in poverty and economic well-being. Publications on its Web site include a collection of technical research reports supplemented by "Frequently Asked Questions About Poverty" and the *Focus* newsletter, which contains shorter essays for the general reader, including "A Primer on U.S. Welfare Reform" and "Rethinking the Safety Net: Gaps and Instability in Help for the Working Poor."

Kaiser Family Foundation
2400 Sand Hill Rd.
Menlo Park, CA 94025
(650) 854-9400
fax: (650) 854-4800
Web site: www.kff.org

The Kaiser Family Foundation is a nonprofit, privately operated foundation focusing on the major health care issues facing the United States, with a growing role in global health. Kaiser develops and runs its own research and communications programs, providing facts, information, and analysis for policy makers, the media, the health care community, and the public, from sophisticated policy research, to basic facts and numbers, to information young people can use to improve their health or elderly people can use to understand their Medicare benefits. Its Web site offers a collection of fact sheets, data and charts, issue briefs, interactive tools, and news releases on such topics as "The Uninsured and the Difference Health Insurance Makes" and "Low-Wage Workers and Health Care."

National Center for Children in Poverty (NCCP)
215 W. 125th St., 3rd Fl.
New York, NY 10027
(646) 284-9600
fax: (646) 284-9623
e-mail: info@nccp.org
Web site: www.nccp.org

Founded in 1989 as a division of the Mailman School of Public Health at Columbia University, the NCCP is a nonpartisan, public interest research organization, dedicated to promoting the economic security, health, and well-being of America's low-income families and children. NCCP uses research to promote family-oriented solutions at the state and national levels. Its Web site's welfare section includes a searchable database of research on welfare reform, profiles of individual state programs, and publications including the reports "Improving Work Supports" and "State Policies Can Promote Immigrant Children's Economic Security."

Poverty and Race Research Action Council (PRRAC)
1015 Fifteenth St. NW, Ste. 400
Washington, DC 20005
(202) 906-8023
fax: (202) 842-2885
e-mail: info@prrac.org
Web site: www.prrac.org

The PRRAC is a civil rights policy organization convened by major civil rights, civil liberties, and antipoverty groups to help connect advocates with social scientists working on race and poverty issues. PRRAC sponsors social science research, provides technical assistance, and convenes advocates and researchers around particular race and poverty issues. Through its Web site and publications, the organization supports public education efforts, producing the bimonthly newsletter *Poverty & Race*, as well as articles and policy briefings on topics including "New Paths for Action Against Racism and Poverty in the United States and All Its Territories."

Urban Institute
2100 M St. NW, Ste. 500
Washington, DC 20037
(202) 833-7200
Web site: www.urban.org

Established in 1968 by President Lyndon Johnson, the Urban Institute gathers data, conducts research, evaluates programs, offers technical assistance overseas, and educates Americans on social and economic issues to foster sound public policy and effective government. The issues on which researchers focus are those with the greatest potential effect on the public, including welfare, health, and education. The institute operates in all fifty states and abroad in over twenty-eight countries, and shares its research findings online and through reports and scholarly books. Online offerings include "Issues in Focus," "Welfare Reform: Ten Years Later," and "Low-Income Working Families."

For Further Reading

Books

Albelda, Randy, and Ann Withorn, eds., *Lost Ground: Welfare Reform, Poverty, and Beyond.* Cambridge, MA: South End, 2002. Fourteen essays by social scientists examining welfare reform as it affects issues of gender and race, and concluding that reform has punished poor people instead of helping them.

Albert, Raymond, and Louise Skolnik, *Social Welfare Programs: Narratives from Hard Times.* Belmont, CA: Thomson, 2006. Intended as an overview for social workers, this volume devotes a chapter to each of six major welfare programs, giving legal background, a description of each program, and first-person accounts from clients.

Bernstein, Jared, *All Together Now: Common Sense for a Fair Economy.* San Francisco: Berrett-Koehler, 2006. A passionate argument from an economist who believes that any new national economy should put economic equality ahead of profits.

Blades, Joan, and Kristin Rowe-Finkbeiner, *The Motherhood Manifesto: What America's Moms Want—and What to Do About It.* New York: Nation, 2006. With personal anecdotes and examples of progressive companies, this book describes economic and social policy changes that would benefit mothers and children.

Brooks, Arthur C., *Who Really Cares: The Surprising Truth About Compassionate Conservatism.* New York: Basic, 2006. Shows the importance of charitable giving, and argues that conservatives, who have stronger families and more consistent church attendance, give more than other groups do.

Browning, Edgar K., *Stealing from Each Other: How the Welfare State Robs Americans of Money and Spirit.* A critique of government spending and the modern welfare state that calls for equal opportunity rather than equal results.

Cabrera, Natasha J., Robert M. Hutchens, and Elizabeth Peters, *From Welfare to Childcare: What Happens to Young Children When Single*

Mothers Exchange Welfare for Work. New York: Routledge, 2006. Describes the changes in child care that occurred after welfare reform, and analyzes the influence of reform on the way children are cared for when their mothers enter the workforce.

Cahn, Edgar, *No More Throw-Away People: The Co-Production Imperative*. Washington, DC: Essential, 2004. Argues that people receiving welfare can become productive change agents, particularly if "work" is redefined to include nonmarket activities such as family care and community building.

Cavoukian, Raffi, and Sharna Olfman, eds., *Child Honoring: How to Turn This World Around*. New York: Praeger, 2006. This collaboration between the children's singer Raffi and a psychologist argues for an economic, social, and political culture that puts the needs of children first.

Currie, Janet, *The Invisible Safety Net: Protecting the Nation's Poor Children and Families*. Princeton, NJ: Princeton University Press, 2006. Proposes a new reform agenda that emphasizes in-kind programs over payments, and calls for improved integration of programs to prevent children from slipping through the cracks.

Daly, Lew, *God and the Welfare State*. Cambridge, MA: MIT Press, 2006. A brief examination of the need for, and the successes and the dangers of, faith-based antipoverty programs.

DeParle, Jason, *American Dream: Three Women, Ten Kids, and a Nation's Drive to End Welfare*. New York: Viking, 2004. Social policy reporter DeParle narrates the lives of three African American women who left the welfare rolls and joined the working poor.

Eisler, Riane, *The Real Wealth of Nations: Creating a Caring Economics*. San Francisco: Berrett-Koehler, 2007. Calls for a radical new economics that values work performed in caring for family, community, and nature.

Handler, Joel F., and Yeheskel Hasenfeld, *Blame Welfare, Ignore Poverty and Inequality*. New York: Cambridge University Press, 2007. Argues that the United States should stop focusing on welfare and welfare reform, and make a new directed effort to eliminate poverty by addressing inequality.

Massaro, Thomas, *United States Welfare Policy: A Catholic Response.* Washington, DC: Georgetown University Press, 2007. Massaro, a Catholic social ethicist, argues that in considering treatment of the poor, Catholics should not consider the cost of programs but rather their effectiveness at preserving the well-being of all.

Murray, Charles, *In Our Hands: A Plan to Replace the Welfare State.* Washington, DC: AEI, 2006. Murray's plan includes eliminating all existing entitlement programs, which he considers harmful, and giving every adult citizen an annual ten-thousand-dollar grant for health insurance, retirement savings, and other expenses.

Nadasen, Premilla, *Welfare Warriors: The Welfare Rights Movement in the United States.* New York: Routledge, 2004. The definitive history of the welfare rights movement, and the feminism that shaped it.

Sered, Susan Starr, and Rushika Fernandopulle, *Uninsured in America: Life and Death in the Land of Opportunity.* An anthropologist and a physician conducted 120 interviews for this look at the dangers and the costs posed to everyone by illness that goes untreated in the uninsured.

Stricker, Frank, *Why America Lost the War on Poverty—and How to Win It.* Chapel Hill: University of North Carolina Press, 2007. Argues that the only way to seriously address poverty is to create good jobs and to focus government resources on low-income workers.

Waltman, Jerold L., *The Case for the Living Wage.* New York: Algora, 2004. Waltman, a political scientist, argues that the living wage would work better than credits, subsidies, or cash payments to ensure the well-being of low-wage workers.

Periodicals

Albeda, Randy, and Heather Boushey, "From Welfare to Poverty," August 23, 2006, TomPaine.com.

Ashburn, Elyse, "New Regulations Could Push More Welfare Recipients Out of College," *Chronicle of Higher Education,* August 11, 2006.

Clinton, Bill, "How We Ended Welfare, Together," *New York Times,* August 22, 2006.

Eckholm, Eric, "Food Stamp Use in U.S. at Record Pace as Jobs Vanish," *New York Times*, March 31, 2008.

————, "For the Neediest of the Needy, Welfare Reforms Still Fall Short, Study Says," *New York Times*, May 17, 2006.

Farrara, Peter J., "Slimming Entitlement Costs," *Barron's*, October 8, 2007.

Flono, Fannie, "Bush Signed Health Insurance Bill That Fails Kids," *Charlotte (NC) Observer*, January 4, 2008.

Garrett, Scott, "Tax-and-Spend Ideology Taints Children's Health Measure," *Bergen County (NJ) Record*, October 23, 2007.

Gragg, Rachel, and Margy Waller, "Welfare Reform, 10 Years Later," *Boston Globe*, August 22, 2006.

Gregory, James, "Poverty from Workhouse to the Welfare State," *History Today*, July 2008.

Haskins, Ron, "Welfare Check," *Wall Street Journal*, July 27, 2006.

Koch, Wendy, "Rules Relaxed for 'Food Stamp' Eligibility," *USA Today*, October 20, 2008.

Lappé, Frances Moore, "Changing Our Minds: Ending Poverty Begins with Fresh Thinking," *Sojourners*, September/October 2008.

Lewis, Anne C., "Addressing Child Well-Being," *Education Digest*, May 2008.

Lott, Deshae, "Medicaid Reform Needed Now," *Quest*, September/October 2005.

Mannes, George, "Why We Have to Cut Benefits for Seniors," *Money*, November 2008.

Mead, Lawrence M., "Crying Poverty," *Commentary*, September 2007.

Murray, Charles, "A Plan to Replace the Welfare State," *Wall Street Journal*, March 26, 2006.

Olson, Sarah, "Marriage Promotion, Reproductive Injustice, and the War Against Women of Color," *Dollars and Sense*, January/February 2005.

O'Shaughnessy, Lynn, "Rising Prices Hammer Seniors on Fixed Incomes," *USA Today*, July 2, 2008.

Pollitt, Katha, "Poverty Is Hazardous to Your Health," *Nation*, September 20, 2007.

Quinn, Jane Bryant, "The Kids Aren't All Right," *Newsweek*, October 29, 2007.

Rector, Robert, "Bill Clinton Was Right: He Saw the Roots of America's Welfare Problem," *Washington Post*, August 23, 2006.

Sapolsky, Robert, "Sick of Poverty," *Scientific American*, December 2005.

Sklar, Holly, "Carving Up Our Economic Pie," Knight Ridder, Tribune Information Services, November 22, 2005.

Spatz, Diana, "Bush Welfare Agenda: Married to a Myth," *Christian Science Monitor*, February 24, 2004.

Swarns, Rachel L., "State Programs Add Safety Net for the Poorest," *New York Times*, May 12, 2008.

Tanner, Michael, "Welfare Reform—What Worked," *San Francisco Chronicle*, August 21, 2006.

Walker, Jesse, "The Amazing Colossal Poorhouse," Reason Online, August 22, 2006.

Walters, Jonathan, "Is Welfare Working?" *Governing*, Fall 2008.

Wayne, Alex, and Drew Armstrong, "The SCHIP Challenge: Finding Funding," *CQ Weekly*, August 6, 2006.

Will, George, "The Right Minimum Wage," *Washington Post*, January 4, 2007.

Wolf, Richard, "New Breed of American Emerges in Need of Food," *USA Today*, May 19, 2008.

Zuckerman, Mortimer B., "Family-Unfriendly Policies," *U.S. News & World Report*, October 15, 2007.

Web sites

kaiserEDU.org (www.kaiseredu.org). Focusing on health care policy, this site for students and teachers includes narrated slide tutorials, background reference libraries, and modules on current topics and debates.

Links to the World: Welfare and Low Income Issues (www.leg.state .mn.us/LRL/links/Welfare.asp). A collection of articles on state and federal issues, and links to public policy organizations, maintained by the Minnesota Legislative Reference Library.

NCCIC Library (www.nccic.org/library/index.cfm?do=oll.search). A searchable federal government site that gathers summaries, articles, reports, and statistics on all aspects of child care.

Public Agenda (www.publicagenda.org). An award-winning site designed to help citizens and leaders gather the information and opinions they need to understand important issues. Includes a "Poverty and Welfare" issue guide.

Index

Roosevelt, Franklin D., 8

Picture Credits

Maury Aaseng, 14, 22, 26, 33, 39, 42, 49, 54, 62, 68, 73, 79, 91, 98, 104, 111, 115

© age fotostock/SuperStock, 106

AP Images, 35, 37, 85

Dennis Brack/Bloomberg News/Landov, 66

Thomas Cain/Getty Images, 60

© Mark Gibson/Alamy, 27

© Jeff Greenberg/Alamy, 93

Ted Jackson/The Times-Picayune/Landov, 47

Stephen Jaffe/Reuters/Landov, 20

© Janine Wiedel Photolibrary/Alamy, 16

Shelly Katz/Liaison/Getty Images, 10

Steve Liss/Time Life Pictures/Getty, 55

© Lyroky/Alamy, 75

© Michael Neelon (misc)/Alamy, 81

© North Wind Picture Archives/Alamy, 31

© Frances Roberts/Alamy, 70

Sami Sarkis/Photographer's Choice/Getty Images, 116

© Trinity Mirror/Mirrorpix/Alamy, 110

© Jim West/Alamy, 97

© Alison Wright/Corbis, 44